Piaget's Theory Applied to an Early Childhood Curriculum

Celia Stendler Lavatelli

University of Illinois

A Center for Media Development, Inc. Book

American Science and Engineering, Inc., Boston • Cambridge

A Center for Media Development, Inc. Book
American Science and Engineering, Inc., Boston • Cambridge
SECOND EDITION

Contents

v

Introduction

THE NAME OF JEAN PIAGET is fast becoming known to millions of Americans. The phenomenon is a recent one. While his writings on language and moral development were widely read in the 30's and early 40's, Piaget's work on intelligence was largely ignored until the very late 50's and the 60's. American psychologists criticized him for lack of hard data; Piaget, they said, only reported what went on in his interviews with children, but did not do statistical research. It is only in the past decade that Piaget has "caught on" in America, and that his tremendous contribution to theory has been recognized.

Piaget was born in Switzerland in 1896, over 70 years ago, and began his productive career while still a child, publishing, at the age of ten, a one-page paper on an albino sparrow he had observed. His early interests were in the biological sciences; he wrote his dissertation on mollusks and published a number of scholarly papers on the subject. However, he was always interested in philosophy and psychology and felt that biology could contribute to the question of how children acquire knowledge. He worked for a time, under Binet in Paris, on standardization of intelligence test items. Intelligence tests require that the child be scored according to specific answers to questions. However, Piaget began asking children to explain answers and became fascinated by their incorrect as well as correct explanations. Later, in Geneva, he observed the spontaneous behavior of his own children and also elicited behavior from them. With co-workers he developed "tasks" in number, space, classification, etc., and recorded children's reasoning about these tasks. He used these careful recordings and observations as supporting evidence for his evolving theory of how intelligence develops.

Today, Piaget is recognized as one of the great theorists in developmental psychology. He has given us a model of processes involved in the acquisition of knowledge and the development of logical intelligence from birth through the adolescent period. A broad spectrum of disciplines draws upon his work: psychology, education, sociology, anthropology, mathematics, etc. Indeed, it is hard to get a degree in an American university today without being exposed to Piaget's work.

Obviously, any theory of how children acquire knowledge should have applications for what might be done to make the acquisition of knowledge more effective. In fact, Piaget himself says that his theory has application to pedagogy, but he also says that he is not a pedagogue and that he leaves the task of application to educators.

This book describes an application of his theories to early childhood curriculum. It reviews relevant aspects of Piaget's theory, describing and explaining how the child acquires classification, number, measurement, space and seriation concepts. It also describes how the theory may be applied to instructional processes for four, five and six-year-old children. The program is designed to help children acquire logical ways of thinking; it provides children with concrete materials upon which to carry out certain actions, and it supplies to the teacher the key questions or problems to ask of children. Piaget contends that it is the action of the subject upon objects or events in the environment that leads to assimilation of new ideas, accommodation of existing mental structures to the new ideas, and establishment of mental equilibrium on a higher level. The concrete materials encourage physical action while the teacher's questions stimulate mental activity.

Putting the program into effect carries with it an unexpected dividend. It results in the teacher becoming much more sophisticated about thinking processes. Piaget is difficult to understand, but his theory becomes meaningful as teachers pose problems for children to solve using the concrete materials, and as the teachers listen to children's explanations and reasoning about the problems. I have seen teachers using the program begin by sticking closely to activities and questions suggested in the text. However, as they hear over and over again the same replies, they begin to be creative about their probing and to suggest problems for children to investigate in connection with block play, doll play and the like. *Telling* children is *not* teaching, as Piaget reminds us. Others do not convince us that we are wrong about our ideas; only we can convince ourselves. But the teacher who knows how to ask the right question at the right time can spark children's own search for answers and stimulate the child to make his own discoveries.

It is impossible to express my debt of gratitude to Professor Piaget, all of whose lectures I followed at the University of Geneva during part of a sabbatical year. This "giant" of epistomology, as Professor J. McVicker Hunt has called him, changed my thinking about the nature of intelligence and opened my eyes to the possibilities of applying his theory to the education of young children. His writings, together with those of Barbel Inhelder, continue to be a source of inspiration to me as well as to thousands of others. My good friend, Mme. Marianne Denis-Prinzhorn of the J. J. Rousseau Institut, was most helpful while I was in Geneva, permitting me to attend the Practicum she was giving in the public schools where I could observe each week the administration of the Piaget tasks, and clearing up my difficulties in understanding.

I am also indebted to my colleagues at the University of Illinois: Professor Queenie Mills, co-director of our preschool project, Mrs. Jean Morris, head teacher, and her assistants, Mrs. Constance Solberg and Mrs. Laurel Hertig; to Mrs. Glenys Unruh, Curriculum Director, and Dr. James Dunlap, Coordinator of Research and Testing, the kindergarten teachers in University City Public Schools, Missouri; and to the teachers in the Children's Centers at Oakland, California, all of whom made it possible for me to observe the effects of training upon children's development.

I should also like to express my thanks to Miss Elise Piquet and Miss Shirley Weese who designed and illustrated the kit materials and books, in the preparation of the program.

And, finally, to Leo, my husband, whose faith in me and encouragement of my professional ventures are a continuing source of strength.

CELIA STENDLER LAVATELLI

University of Illinois
May 1970

Herb Weitman, University City Public Schools, University City, Missouri

The question of a structured versus a nonstructured program is one that plagues many preschool teachers. While unstructured programs predominated for many years, some experimental curricula have recently swung to the opposite extreme of a completely structured day. In the Piagetian curriculum described in this book, structured activities are carried on during one period of the day, leaving the balance for free play, creative arts, music and stories. The daily structured period gives the teacher the opportunity to expose all children to specific types of cognitive training, while the unstructured part affords opportunities for application and reinforcement of the cognitive skills. In connection with a conservation of surface area activity shown here, children receive training in such logical operations as reversing a process and putting parts together in different ways to form a whole.

1. Contrasting Views of Early Childhood Education*

THE PAST DECADE has seen a revolutionary change in thinking about the development of intelligence. From a point of view where intelligence was regarded as a fixed, unchanging product of heredity, we now view mental capacity at a particular point in time as the result of the *interaction* of heredity and experience.

This is not a restatement of the popular generalization that both heredity and environment affect intellectual development. Nor is it a restatement of the notion that one is born with a particular intellectual capacity, but whether or not that capacity develops depends upon environment. The interactional point of view is that mental structures develop from infancy as the result of encounters with the environment, and that the changes are *cumulative*. The behavior of an individual in a particular encounter, the way in which he solves a problem, depends upon the mental structures built out of earlier interactions which depend, in turn, upon structures built in still earlier interactions. In particular, in the interactional school of thought, the early childhood years are regarded as critical. There is a growing realization that the kind of experi-

---

* A shorter version of this chapter appeared as a paper in *Childhood Education*, February, 1970. The material is used here with permission of the Association for Childhood Education International, Washington, D.C.

ences with which the young child has a chance to interact affects the development of his intelligence, and a conviction that the young child should be provided with experiences that will stimulate his thinking and contribute to the growth of mental structures.

CHANGING VIEWS OF INTELLIGENCE

The changing view of intelligence as something that grows with stimulation is partly the result of Dr. Hunt's book, *Intelligence and Experience* in which he reviewed research of several decades on environmental impact upon intelligence test scores. Some of the research involved animal studies; some human subjects. One particularly dramatic study involved the effects of stimulation in infancy upon later intellectual development. The question asked was, would a group of babies reared under conditions of minimum stimulation be handicapped in intellectual development as compared with babies raised in a stimulating environment? While we cannot deliberately subject human beings to conditions that we suspect might be bad for them, it has been possible in the past to find babies living in institutions under conditions of minimum stimulation. Skeels and Dye (1939) described such babies they had found in an orphanage in a practically vegetable state of existence—listless, dull, withdrawn, inactive. The babies were receiving excellent physical care but little stimulation in the way of social play or toys from busy caretakers. The psychologists were so concerned about the viability of three of these infants, in particular, that they took them out of the orphanage and put them in the only other available institution—a home for mentally retarded girls. There, the three babies were cared for by fourteen-year-olds selected as somewhat brighter than average among the feeble-minded inmates. Several months later, when the psychologists were visiting the same institution, they were struck with the bright, alert, intelligent behavior of three infants whom they found there. They were astonished to discover that these were the three listless babies placed in the care of the mentally retarded girls some time before. What had happened was that the fourteen-year-olds took a motherly interest in the babies and showered them with attention missing in the orphanage where the infants had spent day after day, in cribs, with little stimulation from people or things. The psychologists decided to test the effects of a more stimulating environment upon 13 additional babies, whose initial test scores were equivalent to from 36 to 89 IQ points. Two years later, an average gain of 27 points on developmental scales was recorded for the group. A follow-up study twenty-one years later showed that the adults who had grown up in the more stimulating environment were self-sustaining adults while those who had remained in the orphanage in infancy were still institutionalized.

From many such researches has come the conviction that intelligence is not fixed but grows. And, as is the case with other growth variables, the effect of the environment is greatest during the period of greatest change for that growth variable. It is during early childhood that cognitive growth is most rapid. One psychologist (Bloom, 1964) has estimated that, when age 17 is taken as the criterion age, some 50% of the total IQ at that age can be predicted at age 4, and an additional 30% from ages four to eight. In other words, curves of mental growth appear to rise rapidly in early childhood and to taper off to a plateau in late adolescence; it is important, therefore, to provide stimulating experiences to stimulate intellectual growth during the early childhood years.

The point of view presented here with respect to stimulating the growth of intelligence has been challenged recently in a paper by Jensen (1969). Jensen argues that environmental factors are not nearly as important in determining IQ as are genetic factors. He arrives at this position partly on the basis of his analysis of genetic and environmental components in intelligence test scores; he finds that the more closely related two people are, the more similar their IQ scores, indicating a strong genetic determinant. Jensen also examines other lines of evidence, including results of attempts to use education to raise the IQ, and concludes that compensatory education has failed; changes in IQ scores produced in such programs have been generally small and fleeting. And, in a still more controversial vein, Jensen summarizes intelligence test and school performance data of Negro children and concludes, "The preponderance of the evidence is, in my opinion, less consistent with a strictly environmental hypothesis than with a genetic hypothesis, which, of course, does not exclude the influence of environment or its interaction with genetic factors" (p. 82).

Although Jensen asserts that educators have minimized or denied the role of heredity, on the contrary, it is fair to say that most educators agree with him that intellectual performance has a genotypic base. But educators are far from convinced that we have provided the best possible environment for the nurturance of intelligence, and they are at the same time convinced that in the case of disadvantaged racial minorities, nurturance in early childhood is so poor that intellectual growth suffers. They disagree with Jensen's statement, "Compensatory education has been tried and it apparently has failed." By and large, educators feel that we have barely begun our efforts to alter the "ecological niche," to use Hunt's apt phrase, of young children. Critical reviews of Jensen's paper (Harvard Educational Review, 1969) by psychologists and educators alike continue to emphasize the importance of quality education in early childhood and the need to develop and evaluate early childhood education programs. Particularly in the case of the disadvantaged is there a need to intervene educationally to counteract the effects of a poor socio-economic environment.

But what form should educational intervention take? What are effective ways of overcoming the intellectual and educational disadvantages of poverty? When should intervention begin? For years, public schools enrolling large numbers of children from deprived backgrounds attacked the problem simply but ineffectually; they planned for the disadvantaged a curriculum one or more grades below the norm. Thus, "slow-learning" fifth graders studied subject matter normally mastered in the third grade, with no expectation on the school's part that they would do more than a year's work in the academic year. Under this too-typical pattern, not only did the children not catch up, but they appeared to lose ground, so that the gap in performance between middle and lower classes increased with each school grade. It is this kind of solution that writers like Kenneth Clark have criticized.

Today, there is a strong tendency to begin educational intervention earlier than entrance into elementary school, and to base the nature of the intervention on the special intellective and motivational deficits revealed by research on the disadvantaged. Experimental preschool programs have been devised to counteract specific cognitive disabilities that are rooted in the child's social background. In the affective realm, certain deficits in achievement motivation are being identified, and special efforts are being made to strengthen the drive to do well in school. It is the aim of this chapter to analyze and evaluate contemporary approaches to educational intervention, and to present the case for a program based upon present knowledge of the origins and development of human intelligence.

The nursery school years have traditionally been regarded as the period when educational intervention into the lives of children of the poor would be most effective. The child is old enough to bear separation from home, yet sufficiently plastic in development so that, with intervention, he can remedy maladaptive behavioral and thought patterns. Left in his deprived environment until entrance into first grade, the disadvantaged child has several years to build up ways of getting along in his environment that may actually interfere with school learning. He develops speech and thought patterns that differ from those he needs to learn the 3 R's. The analogy is sometimes made to an adult moving to a new city. Unless he builds a comprehensive map of the city in his mind within the first few weeks, he will find other, less efficient, ways of getting about; after several years, he may discover that he does not really know the geography of the city. In the same way, children of the poor must build thought patterns conducive to school learning as early as possible. A considerable amount of interesting experimentation is now in progress to help all children do exactly that.

TYPES OF EARLY CHILDHOOD CURRICULA

The Child-Development Oriented Nursery School

The child-development oriented nursery school, or traditional nursery school, as it has come to be called, has placed emphasis upon the child's social and emotional development, perhaps more than upon his intellective development. This is understandable since the school population is largely middle-class, and middle-class parents typically provide their children with an intellectually stimulating environment. Nursery school teachers have been trained to study child behavior, to search for unconscious motivations, and to direct the activity of the child in order to shape his behavior constructively. The overly-aggressive child has been restrained and redirected, and the reasons he should refrain from aggression have been explained to him. The overdependent child has been helped to wean himself from home and mother and to grow in self-reliance. At the same time, teachers have emphasized social adjustment and have helped children acquire habits of consideration for the feelings of others, of working constructively with others, of taking responsibility for finishing activities and cleaning-up, of sharing equipment and taking turns. Parent-teacher conferences have eased problems of over-controlled behavior, poor eating habits, sibling rivalry, thumbsucking, and bed-wetting.

The development of creativity has been a major concern of the pre-school curriculum. Large building blocks, a housekeeping corner, dress-up clothes, paints, and clay have been traditional items of equipment in nursery schools, and children have used them freely and imaginatively, with few restrictions or directions for use. In fact, most nursery school programs include a large block of time in which children can engage in free play, choosing what they want to play with and what they want to do as they play. Building with blocks may take the form of constructing an airport, and a child may then practice take-offs and landings with his "jets." In doll play, a child may be "mother" to a baby doll, perhaps alternately loving and spanking the "infant." Such play has been advocated not only for its contribution to the development of creativity, but also for its tension-releasing effects. An overcontrolled child may gradually become more happy and relaxed as he dabbles in fingerpaints, and a child plagued by jealousy over a baby sister can express his feelings by spanking a baby doll rather than repressing hostility and feeling guilty.

While personality development, social adjustment, and creativity have received the major emphasis in traditional programs, other aspects of development have not been neglected. Teachers have been taught to be concerned with motor coordination, and to provide many opportunities for large muscle activity on wheel toys, swings, jungle gyms and imaginative substitutes for traditional equipment. They have been concerned about language development, and have used storytelling, show-and-tell periods, and free time to build vocabulary, to improve pronunciation and grammar, and to encourage the non-talker to speak. They have planned trips to expand the child's social horizons and have raised plants and animals in the playroom to develop his powers of observation and increase his knowledge of science.

Preschool programs for children from both middle and low socio-economic groups reflected and continue to reflect social-emotional goals to some extent. The school day usually begins with a period of free-choice activity during which the child may work as he chooses, with blocks, doll-play equipment, wheel toys, art media, puzzles or games. During this period, the teacher and assistants observe and interact with the children, steering their play and social activity into constructive channels as the need arises, encouraging the shy and timid, and redirecting the boisterous and aggressive. There follows a cleanup time where each child must take responsibility for putting away equipment he has been using and cleaning up whatever mess he may have made. Time is also provided in the day for a snack of juice or milk, where there is considerable emphasis upon social conversation; for outdoor play, where big muscle activity is encouraged; for music, rhythms, and stories; and for a rest period to avoid overfatigue and overstimulation. The role of the teacher in all of these activities is to *guide* children's behavior and development; children are allowed considerable freedom to explore the possibilities in equipment, to use it creatively either alone or with others, and to develop *their* potential at *their* own rate.

Not all nursery schools and kindergartens allow such freedom. There are many where children trace patterns, color outlines with prescribed colors, engage in reading readiness activities often involving workbooks, and where, in general, the preschool is seen as a miniature first grade. Play is de-emphasized, and so is freedom of movement. Children spend most of their time in their seats working on quiet activities. The child development theorists, as might be expected, were and continue to be extremely critical (and rightly so) of programs that offer little in the way of social-emotional-cognitive growth for children. Such stereotyped curricula offer no serious challenge to the child development point of view.

After reading the favorable picture of the child-development oriented preschool, the reader may be shocked to discover that this type of preschool is under severe attack. Criticism of early school education is not new; for years, both kindergartens and nursery schools have been urged to include the 3 R's in their programs in order to prepare the child for first grade. The attacks today, are of a different nature. It is not that the preschool is being urged to add something to its curriculum, but rather that the total curriculum is under fire by educational psychologists, sociologists, and popular writers. The preschool is being accused not merely of *neglecting* intellectual development but, since it disapproves of formal teaching, of actually being *anti*-intellectual. The accusation has been made that keeping intellectual content from the child and not forcing him prematurely into formal learning denies him the stimulation that would help his mind grow. The argument goes further; not only does such an anti-intellectual curriculum fail to meet the special needs of young, disadvantaged children, say the critics, but it is not even desirable for middle-class children. Such critics speak contemptuously of the emphasis placed upon personal-social adjustment through permissive play and the lack of emphasis on cognitive activities.

However, such criticism should not blind us to the considerable contribution play activities make to intellective development. Every serious student in the field has pointed out that the play of the child is not just random activity, but involves considerable directed experimentation. Balancing a seesaw, building a block tower, floating play toys, putting away play toys by categories, pouring juice into containers of different sizes—these are examples of play activities from which new information can be assimilated, developing mental structures accommodated, and new behavior patterns emerge. Were all nursery school teachers and psychological investigators as alert as Piaget (1951) to the contribution of play to cognition, there might be more exploitation of its educational possibilities.

Montessori preschools

The first serious challenge to the child development point of view came with the rebirth of the Montessori movement. Nursery schools based upon Montessori pedagogy mushroomed in the 50's and 60's. These schools differed from the prevailing nursery school in that there was a great deal of structure to activities, and that there was little emphasis upon social-emotional development.

Perhaps education of the senses has become more synonymous with Montessori's philosophy than any other facet. Montessori believed in deliberate sensory training, and planned exercises and equipment designed to make tactile, thermic, baric (weight) and muscular senses more acute. Didactic materials were prepared, for example, to teach children to recognize various Euclidean shapes— square, rectangle, circle, polygon, ellipse, etc., by inserting each into the appropriately shaped hole in a large frame. Other equipment, like letters of the alphabet made out of sandpaper, taught children the shape of the letters and eventually led to reading experiences.

Another aspect of the Montessori curriculum is the teaching of skills to enable the child to be independent. These were the "Exercises of Practical Life," (discussed in her books, particularly in *The Montessori Method,* Cambridge, Mass., Robert Bentley Inc., 1964) and included such activities as buttoning and unbuttoning buttons on a chart, practice in tying shoelaces, pouring water from a pitcher, dusting, sweeping, and caring for equipment. While many of the exercises seem dated today—and indeed, one of the criticisms of the Montessori movement is that its curriculum and equipment were based upon the needs of the slum child in Rome at the turn of the century—it may be that the "Exercises of Practical Life," although designed to teach freedom through discipline, served another purpose. As we have noted, Montessori reports that the exercises were thoroughly enjoyed by the children who spent long hours over them with no urging by the teacher. Psychologists like Piaget have called attention to the repetitive quality of the infant's behavior. Piaget has noted that during the first year of life, a baby will repeat an activity over and over again; having just discovered how to make "an interesting sight last," he puts his discovery to work. Three-year-olds, however, have to get more out of a task to stay with it a long time. It may be that the great appeal of the "Exercises" lay in the intellectual stimulation they provided. Tying knots may lead to some important topological concepts; pouring liquids into various shaped receptacles may aid the child to see that the amount of a substance is conserved regardless of a change in its shape. The intense interest of a child might be explained not so much by his satisfaction in being able to button a button by himself, but by the satisfaction of his intellectual curiosity about how buttons "work."

Today's psychologist is very much concerned with the problems of intrinsic motivation. Montessori, unwittingly, hit upon one way to provide for it. What we need to ask today is, what kind of equipment will provoke a child's curiosity and at the same time develop his intelligence? Is there a better way than the "Exercises of Practical Life?" Knowledge of cognitive development has advanced considerably from the days of Montessori. Thanks to investigators like Piaget, we ought to do better than the "Exercises."

One of the strengths of the Montessori program lay in its power to *motivate* the child to learn. Given materials that were challenging and self-teaching, the child would spend long periods of time with them. He might arrange cylinders in a series, for example, and in the process acquire some notions of how objects can be ordered in terms of height and thickness, or both. In one instance, Montessori herself observed a child remove and replace the cylinders 44 times! This zest for learning through self-activity is important to keep in mind in planning programs for young children. It is what Hunt has called "intrinsic motivation." Children will keep at a task for long periods of time, provided they are getting something out of the task. What Montessori demonstrated is that finding out something new for oneself is rewarding and hence motivating.

Enrichment Programs

Enrichment programs are generally planned to add to the traditional curriculum activities designed to overcome specific cognitive and affective deficits in disadvantaged children. Unfortunately, little evaluative information is available for most enrichment programs, and where data are reported, the kind of enrichment provided is not described in sufficient detail to be helpful to others. An exception is the intervention program of Deutsch and others at the Institute for Developmental Studies in New York City (1967).

In the ongoing research and demonstration programs of the Institute, experimental subjects are exposed to an enriched curriculum beginning with two years of pre-first grade and continuing through the third grade. Most of the children are Negro, and all share the same socio-economic background in Harlem.

For the enrichment classes, the physical environment of the typical nursery school with housekeeping, block, art and book centers has been expanded to include a number of auto-instructional devices. One of these, the *Listening Center*, accommodates six children at a time; they listen on individual earphones to tapes recorded first in the teacher's voice, and then in a variety of voices and language styles not found in the home environment. Tapes may require only listening on the part of the child, or they may require motor or verbal responses. Each of the two types is designed to foster a particular kind of learning, and they are sequenced for presentation. There is also a *Language Master*, a two-track tape recorder with the teacher's voice recorded as a standard on one track to which the child can compare his own recording on the other track. A visual stimulus can be presented at the same time. Additional special materials for visual discrimination include an Alphabet Board with cutouts in the shape of letters of the alphabet into which children put the appropriate letter which will fit only the proper slot. A talking typewriter (the Edison Responsive Environment instrument) is also being used to aid reading acquisition. Emphasis in all the materials is upon the presentation of stimuli in an orderly sequence.

The curriculum for experimental subjects is a "therapeutic curriculum." Language training does not occur in isolated periods; rather, all class activities are used to expose the child to acceptable verbal patterns and to insist upon his using language as a means of social and self-communication. Vocabulary for dealing with concepts of size, shape, color, number, space, time, and temperature is taught as children engage in activities involving these concepts. Special songs in the music period teach children to follow directions ("Put your Finger in the Air") and to discriminate between colors. In general, a three-stage sequence of learning is observed. The first is sensorimotor where contact with concrete materials is provided; the second is a perceptual stage where contrasting stimuli (of colors, shapes, sounds, etc.) are presented; the third is the ideational-representational, where the child deals with objects and ideas with a minimum of concrete and perceptual support.

Evaluation procedures included the use of three standardized tests: the Stanford-Binet, the Peabody Picture Vocabulary Test, and the Columbia Mental Maturity Scale. These standardized tests were administered to the first experimental and control groups at the beginning of the project and again toward the end of the first treatment year. Results on the CMMS are inconclusive. On the Stanford-Binet, no significant differences between groups were found in intelligence test scores at the beginning of the project; both groups tested at about 99 IQ. Differences *were* significant at the .01 level on post-test scores; after a year of schooling, the average IQ for the experimental prekindergarten group on the post-test was 102, while that of the controls was 93. Tests were repeated during the kindergarten year; the *E*'s now tested at almost 104, while the *C*'s had dropped a point to 92.

Essentially the same results were noted for the second groups admitted to the program; children exposed to the enriched curriculum were able to maintain or increase their achievement level, while the mean performance of children left in the poor environment deteriorated. The deterioration at this early age is not significant, but it is worth noting that it *does* become significant after an additional year. Children who entered public school at first-grade level, without any prior schooling, scored significantly lower than did the controls with kindergarten experience, lending further evidence to the hypothesis of a cumulative deficit in IQ scores the longer a child remains in a culturally disadvantaged environment.

Results on the Peabody Picture Vocabulary Test also favored the enriched curriculum. After one year of prekindergarten enrichment, the mean raw score of the *E*'s was significantly higher than that of the *C*'s (44.9 as compared with 37.9). A year later, scores were 52.8 as compared with 48.2, a difference significant at the .05 level.

Enrichment, at least of the Deutsch variety, is yielding measurable gains in IQ scores that hold up over at least a few years. Furthermore, these gains are occurring while children with no schooling or with exposure only to conventional kindergartens are losing ground. Exact mental ages cannot be figured from published data, but if the post-test in the Deutsch project was given about nine months after project initiation, then the children gained about 13 months in mental age during that period. If children were to continue to progress at that rate, they would gain approximately three years of mental age for roughly every two years of chronological growth. Of course, one would expect rate of gain to slow down after a time; the question is whether the accelerated rate can be continued long enough.

For those looking for a model to follow, there is another difficulty inherent in enrichment programs. When a program is "enriched" in many ways, it is never clear which aspects of the curriculum contributed most to the gains, and which were worth very little. If we are to facilitate development of the culturally disadvantaged child to a maximum degree, it becomes necessary to specify the environmental events antecedent to the gains; only as the stimulus is clearly defined can we be confident of our guidelines. Several experimental approaches in which the stimuli have been clearly defined will now be reviewed.

Academically-oriented preschools

The next serious challenge to the prevailing point of view regarding early childhood education came from educational psychologists who were interested in cognitive development (how the child acquires knowledge), and in seeing what could be done to speed up acquisition of academic skills. O.K. Moore (1968) experimented successfully with a "talking typewriter" to see if children as young as two years could learn pre-reading skills. Fowler (1962) reported on teaching the alphabet and sounds of letters to children under two years in an effort to speed up reading acquisition. Bereiter and Engelmann (1966) ran a school for four-year-old disadvantaged children like a high school, with the children moving from class to class for formal lessons in arithmetic, pre-reading skills and language. Programs mushroomed, with each investigator attempting to demonstrate that the early childhood years could and should be used to teach the young child academic skills formerly reserved for the primary grades.

The challenge to the prevailing viewpoint had another facet. Many of those who advocated the teaching of academic skills to the preschool child attacked the "child developmentalists," that is, those who had long argued for education of the *whole child*. Writers like Bereiter and Engelmann accused the "child developmentalists" of being soft and sentimental, of basing theory on outdated mental-hygiene concepts derived from Freud and, worse still, of deliberately cheating the child out of an adequate preschool education. The *whole-child* advocates countered, in turn, by accusing the educational psychologists of misstating their position and of proposing an alternative curriculum hastily devised and tried out, with little regard for its possible negative effects, including the development of overconformity, rigidity of thinking and suppression of creativity.

The situation has been further complicated by America's recently awakened concern for the disadvantaged* and a realization that the many school failures in this group were due in large part to environmental deficiency in the early years. Often, disadvantaged children grow up in homes where there are no pencils, books, crayons, pictures or toys. In fact, there are few objects for them to look at, grasp, or play with, and in so doing to build notions of space, matter and causality out of which intelligence develops. And when language begins, deficit is piled upon deficit, with the result that the child, at school entrance, is severely handicapped in learning what the school wants to teach him.

If controversy rages over what is good preschool education for middle-class children, there is even fiercer controversy over the prerequisites for good compensatory programs. The educational psychologist camp has its own prescription. They would throw out the

---

* A word should be inserted about who the "disadvantaged" are. These children are not necessarily black, Puerto Rican, Indian or Mexican-American. In all of these ethnic groups, and in geographic regions like Appalachia, there are middle and upper-class families whose children are not educationally disadvantaged when they begin school. Some children in working-class families are. They may come from stable homes where a steady income is assured, but educational level of both parents is low. Consequently, intellectual stimulation may be low and the children handicapped as a result. Probably *all* children in lower-lower class homes and particularly those where family life is disorganized can be considered to be culturally and educationally disadvantaged.

traditional preschool program and institute in its place a curriculum to teach academic skills. They argue that a compensatory program should be based upon an analysis of the needs of children. A compensatory language program, for example, would not begin with the language the child already possesses since it is so grossly inadequate for clear, logical thought; it would, instead, teach the child a different language. The child would be taught sentence patterns as if he were learning a second language; these patterns would provide the basis for clear expression about logical relationships and number concepts. Such relationships as "bigger than," "the darkest," "inside the box," and "two comes after one" would be taught by rote, with the child responding to appropriate questions from the teacher.

THE SWING OF THE PENDULUM

In time, however, an uneasy feeling began to stir among the educational psychologists, and, as so often happens when a point of view diverges to the opposite extreme from the prevailing one, the pendulum began to swing back. The pro-academic-skills advocates began to have second thoughts about *not* reading stories to children and *not* encouraging preschoolers to use books. Equipment, like blocks, that had been held up to scorn were suddenly found to have cognitive implications, as experimenters discovered that categories such as large and small, square and triangle, could be easily taught as children replaced blocks on the appropriate shelf after use. Paints and other creative media found their way back into classrooms as these investigators began to find value in such outlets for children's creative expression.

Similarly, many of those who had argued for a relatively unstructured curriculum, where cognitive learnings would be imbedded in the play, music and other activities of the preschool, also began to have second thoughts about whether or not disadvantaged children would catch up in such a program. They began to think that at least part of the day should be structured so the child could engage in compensatory experiences especially designed to overcome environmental deficits. At the same time, there were some misgivings about the adequacy of the traditional program for middle-class children. In an affluent America, many of the activities, kinds of equipment and play experiences provided in preschool are also provided in the home. The question arises, then, as to what kind of preschool education might be planned for middle-class children, with challenging activities over and above what is already available to these children.

Also, it is being recognized that play has not been exploited for its cognitive value. True, the many play activities in nursery school and kindergarten do offer *opportunities* for cognitive growth, as we can observe. Consider a four-year-old playing with blocks in a nursery school. He takes the longest block in the set from the shelf and stands it on the floor. Then he searches for and quickly finds four shorter blocks to pile one on top of the other, making a tower exactly as high as the first. The concept involved here is unit iteration, the essence of measurement. To measure anything, we decide on a standard unit and repeat the unit as often as is necessary. Also involved is the notion that the whole is composed of a number of parts; we can put parts together to equal the whole with which we started. Such concepts are the basis of mathematical understanding and will provide a more solid footing for primary arithmetic than whatever is acquired when the teacher asks of four-year-olds, "What comes after one?", to which question the children chorus an answer, "Two comes after one."

The British Infant School

A movement that does recognize the value of play and is attracting considerable attention on this side of the Atlantic at the present time is that of the British Infant School. Infant schools are government-supported (public) schools enrolling children from five to seven or eight years of age. The classes, of 40 children each, are characterized by informal methods; the children work in small groups, fives, sixes, and sevens in the same room, with older ones teaching younger ones. Learning is individual; classrooms abound with all kinds of materials, and as children work with the materials, they grow in basic knowledge. For example, in the area of mathematics, it is expected that by seven years of age, children will be able, among other things, to classify things into sets, to know the number line and understand place value, to invent their own units of measure or use standard ones, to understand the meaning of addition, subtraction, multiplication, and division, to work problems of shape and size including some simple proportions. Observers comment on the fundamental nature of what the children have learned. One American observer comments, "What the children know, they know for sure; they have time in which to establish an understanding of extremely basic things that are seldom even thought of in American classrooms. First-grade teachers in this country are sometimes astounded to discover how many of the children successfully solving workbook sums have no appreciation of, say, the conservation of a number." (Featherstone, 1968, p. 11).

Science is another area where fundamental learnings go on at a rapid pace. Again, the emphasis is on materials of an open-ended kind that give children freedom to use them in a variety of ways. Containers of various sizes and shapes are available, and as children pour water or sand from one to another, they eventually discover that quantity is conserved even with a change in the shape of the container. There are pets and plants in every classroom to encourage careful operation and experimentation. For example, children might clock the speed of a pet tortoise moving across the playground and note his means of locomotion.

Reading and writing skills go together. There are no formal lessons in these skills, but children make amazing progress in the two or three years they spend in the infant school. There are books in profusion, and children spend considerable time in the library corner before they begin to read. They seem to "pick up" reading as they hang around the library, looking at pictures in books, trying to find words they know, listening as the teacher hears other children read, asking classmates for words they want to know. As the teacher works with an individual or small group, she uses a variety of methods: sight reading, phonics, or whatever seems to work with a child.

Reading and writing are learned simultaneously. When he starts school, the child is given a large, unlined notebook to put in it what he pleases. He may draw a picture, and as he tells the teacher about it, she may write down a word or phrase of what he says. He then makes a copy of the caption just underneath the teacher's. In this way, he comes to know the look and sound of his dictated words and phrases, and begins to enter the words in his own private dictionary as he learns them. Accuracy and neatness, as well as spelling, punctuation and grammar are introduced gradually as ways to say more efficiently what one wants to say.

Art materials are provided, and art experiences are an important part of the school day for every child. So are dramatic play and music, as is true in American preschools. Classrooms, halls and playgrounds, all of which are used freely, are equipped with housekeeping corners, dress-up clothes, sand tables, wood-working benches, and the like, basic equipment resembling that of our own nursery schools.

The British infant schools differ from our kindergartens and first grades in their informality. Children are not assigned to a particular seat in the classroom. Rather, centers are set up, for mathematics, science, reading and writing, dramatics, and other types of activities. After a brief planning session, where the teacher lists the different activities available, small groups go to the various centers and, thereafter, move about on their own, talking quite freely as they do so. The day is literally free for children to use as they wish, with the teacher circulating among them, encouraging, motivating, discussing, helping, prodding. Not all schools have a completely free day; some teachers, especially as they make the change from a formal, rigid program, begin with a free period, gradually extending it as they gain confidence that children can and do learn with the new methods.

How do the schools differ from our own child-centered nursery schools? These, after all, are set up with various activity centers, and children are free to choose what they want to do. Our nursery schools, of course, serve a younger age group—threes, fours, and fives, typically, rather than the fives and sixes of the infant schools. But if one considers the case of a five-year-old in each type of school, one sees certain differences.

In Britain, the five-year-old spends the day with sixes and sevens, as well as with his own age group, whereas our preschools maintain age-grouping. In the so-called "family" or vertical grouping, younger children have many opportunities to learn from older, and vice versa. In addition, the structure of the British school and choice of activities provide for more opportunities to acquire concepts in math, science, and reading and writing skills. Furthermore, the math and science curriculums have some structure to them. In math, for example, activities are grouped around topics: speed, weights and measures, area, volume, etc. A teacher may use assignment cards. A card might ask, "How many acorns balance the pebble?" or "How many bolts balance nine beans?" Some assignment cards are to be worked individually, while others require cooperation of a group of children to complete.

In general, there is more emphasis upon cognitive learnings, and more materials are provided that will encourage cognitive learnings, than is true in progressive preschools in our country that enroll five-year-old children. The theoretical basis is derived largely from Piaget; there is a strong belief that telling is not teaching, and that, as children use good, open-ended materials, their intelligence grows, and basic concepts develop.

The revolution in Britain has much to offer that is interesting and relevant to American teachers. While there are individual differences in teacher competence and success with the newer methods, the methods are demonstrating that children can and do solve complex problems and acquire fundamental knowledge when schools are set up to foster individual learning. Standardized tests show that the children in formal classes do slightly better in achievement than do the children in informal classes; in particular they do better in arithmetic. But the standardized examinations test the ability to compute, which children in formal classes are trained to do; they do not test basic mathematical knowledge which the informal classes stress. Perhaps the newer-type tests being developed by Educational Testing Service will provide an assessment of growth in basic knowledge more suited to the newer methods.

A fundamental difference between our child-centered schools and the infant schools is that play is more explicitly used for cognitive growth in the British system. Most educators recognize that the *opportunities* for cognitive growth are present in play activities, but *not all children* realize them. Some children play with blocks and make no discoveries that have mathematical significance. Some children play in the doll corner and make no discoveries that aid in classifying. Some children take in more information than do others, and thus grow faster in concept acquisition. Part of the difficulty is that the teacher hasn't been trained to appreciate the cognitive content of play, and so she cannot make the fullest use of it.

A solution that is gaining favor in early childhood education in this country is to have the best of the two possible worlds: to use part of the school day (or half-day) for structured, directed-learning activities and the rest of the day for relatively free activities. Directed learning activities are conducted in small groups, with a teacher or assistant working with five or six children for short periods of time. The concepts children acquire during the structured learning periods are reinforced during play as the teacher directs children's observations to phenomena that might otherwise be missed. The teacher is aware of the cognitive implications in play because of the insight into cognitive growth that she has gained in the structured learning activities. For example, she can use the housekeeping corner to teach classification because she knows what is involved in classifying and what children's misconceptions are likely to be.

But what should be the theoretical basis upon which the teacher will select activities that have cognitive content? There must be sound *theory* for intelligent selection; otherwise structured activities could degenerate into busy work, and what the teacher saw as cognitive implications of play could appear trivial.

The best source of theory today on how intelligence develops is Piaget. Jean Piaget is a Swiss psychologist who has been studying, for over 40 years, the development of intelligence in children from birth to adolescence. His writings have provided tremendous insight into the thinking processes of children. From his work the teacher of young children can trace the development of concepts, and upon his theory a sound curriculum in early childhood education can be based. Chapter 2 is devoted to a review of some of the major facets of his theory, and an application of his philosophy to the preschool curriculum.

Short, structured periods can be scheduled in the preschool day when children engage in activities designed to foster logical operations. Here children work on a one-to-one correspondence task: *How to establish the equivalence of two sets of objects or events?* The sure way is to set up a correspondence between individual objects in each set, matching each object in one set with an object in the second set. Here children use physical correspondence to match cups and spoons; they insert in each cup a spoon taken from an extended row of spoons to determine whether the two sets of objects are equivalent. A single activity with one set of materials is not likely to make children logical thinkers, but such a structured activity serves the purpose of focusing the attention of children and teacher on a particular operation and alerts both to opportunities to use that operation throughout the day.

2. Piaget's Developmental Theory and the Preschool Curriculum

PIAGET'S THEORY is a *developmental* one. Thinking processes change during childhood, and the thinking of a four-year-old is *qualitatively* very different from the thinking of a fourteen-year-old. It isn't simply that the older child *knows* more; he does different things with what he knows. Piaget describes the changes in age-related stages. On the basis of his theory, we can predict the thought processes of children within a certain age range. There are, of course, individual differences in maturity of thinking; some children, because of heredity and experience, are more advanced than others, but, according to Piaget, the thinking of all children tends to go through the same stages, and generally when they are at about the same age.

DEVELOPMENTAL STAGES IN PIAGET'S THEORY

The origins of intelligence are to be found in what Piaget calls the *sensorimotor* stage which begins at birth, (Piaget, 1952). The infant comes into the world with two kinds of reflexes: those like the knee jerk that are not altered by experience, and others, like grasping and sucking, that are modified as the infant exercises them. The modification occurs through assimilation and accommodation. For example, the infant accommodates the grasping reflex to the shape of the object to be grasped, curving the fingers in one way for a long, narrow object, and in a different way for a plastic

27

play ring. Later, looking and grasping become coordinated; the infant can put out his hand and grasp that which he sees. Each newly discovered experience brings with it a need to repeat the experience; activity begets activity. And as the infant operates upon the physical world with his sensorimotor system, he acquires notions of objects, space, time, and causality. Ask a ten-month-old baby, "Where's Mommy?" and he looks toward the door through which Mommy has just disappeared; he "thinks" about the concepts of time and objects with his motor system, i.e., Mommy was here but is not now. However, she still exists. Objects have a permanence and do not cease to exist when out of sight.

During the sensorimotor period, the infant lays the foundation for later representational thought. Structures are built which are essential for the mental operations carried on at a later stage of development. The sensorimotor foundations of one structure that adults recognize most easily is that involved in orienting ourselves in space. A person giving directions to a motorist will often turn his body and put out his hands as he "thinks" with his motor system which way to direct the questioner. With a mental map, the need for a motor accompaniment to thinking disappears; thought has become representational. But the structures which enable the school child to deal with space are laid in the sensorimotor period. The concept of a grid system, of an object being displaced in both horizontal and vertical direction, has its primitive beginnings in infant actions (see Table 1).

Gradually, actions become internalized; the child can represent in thought processes that which was first developed on the sensorimotor system. This second stage begins at eighteen months and extends to seven years of age (roughly). The stage is called *preoperational*, for logical operations have not yet appeared. During the early part of this stage (18 months to 4 years), language is developing at a fantastically rapid pace. Furthermore, thought and language are becoming interrelated; from thinking only in images, the child now thinks in words. He can express his ideas in words and can understand the communications of others.

We do not know very much about the early part of this stage for it has not been studied systematically, but Piaget has contributed enormously to our knowledge of development from the age of four years onward. He and his colleagues at Geneva employ what they call the *clinical method* to study development. The examiner presents the child with one of the many cognitive tasks developed at Geneva to study the development of intelligence. The examiner is interested in finding out how the child thinks about the problem, in order to determine how mental processes essential to logical thinking are developing. Therefore the child is asked not only to perform a task but to explain what he is doing and why he is doing it. In questioning the child, the examiner does not employ an interview schedule with every question worked out in advance. Rather, succeeding questions must be phrased in terms of what the child has already said, much as any clinical interview would be conducted. From an analysis of responses, the characteristics of children at each stage of development become known. For example, the child at the pre-operational level (before logical operations have emerged) is likely to think that an object weighs more if its shape has changed. If one of two identical balls of clay is elongated while the child looks on, he thinks that the elongated shape now has more "stuff" in it and weighs more. He judges in terms of how things look to him and centers on *one* variable, length, because length stands out more than does thickness. The child lacks the ability to carry on a mental operation that Piaget calls reversibility—reversing a process mentally to compare what is now with what was.

The thinking of the child at the pre-operational level (4 to 7 years), may be described as follows:

1. The child is perceptually oriented; he makes judgments in terms of how things *look* to him. Piaget has shown that perceptual judgment enters into the child's thinking about matter, space, time, number and causality. For example, the child at the pre-operational level is likely to think that the number of objects in a set changes if the objects are bunched together rather than spread out.

2. The child *centers* on one variable only, usually the variable that stands out visually. He lacks the ability to coordinate variables. In the clay problem described above, length stands out more than does thickness, and the child fails to coordinate the change in length with the change in thickness.

TABLE 1. SOME ASPECTS OF COGNITIVE DEVELOPMENT FROM 0 TO 2 YEARS*

	Sensorimotor intelligence	Object	Play: more assimilation than accommodation	Imitation: more accommodation than assimilation
Stage I (0-1 month)	Birth-reflexes: a) sucking b) grasping c) ocular movements — Three types of assimilation already can be observed: *Reproductive* assiml.: functional exercise, repetition *Recognitory* assiml.: discrimination of situations *Generalizing* assiml.: extension of the reflexes to new objects.	No permanent object. Objects are not distinguished from the act of assimilating them.	"Empty" accommodations free sucking movements: functional play.	Infant is stimulated to cry by hearing other babies cry.
Stage II (1-4 months)	First acquired adaptations and primary circular reactions. Constitution of first habits.	No permanent object. Objects are not distinguished from the act of assimilating them.	Prim. circular reactions sometimes pursued for sheer pleasure.	Imitation only if model starts by imitating child. Model's action treated by child as one of his own actions.

* From a summary by Marianne Denis-Prinzhorn.

	Sensorimotor intelligence	Object	Play: more assimilation than accommodation	Imitation: more accommodation than assimilation
Stage III (4-8 months)	Secondary circular reactions and proceedings for making interesting sights last. Coordination of vision and prehension. Interest in new objects centered on their utilization and not on objects as such.	Object is still a mere extension of child's action: a) anticipation of movements. b) searching movements only for objects child was grasping. c) deferred circ. reaction. d) anticipation of whole object on the basis of seeing part of it. e) child removes obstacle from his face to free his perception.	Sec. circular reactions for sheer pleasure. Assimilatory play becomes more distinct from "serious" adaptation.	Imitation of sounds and movements that already belong to child's repertory and only if child can see or hear his own actions.
Stage IV (8-12 months)	Coordination of secondary schemes and their application to new situations. Distinction between means and goals: *first intentional behaviors.* a) Setting aside an obstacle. b) Use of signs to anticipate events. c) Exploration of new objects with interest centered on objects as such.	Active search for hidden objects. But permanence is still bound to action: if hidden in two successive places child searches at initial place and not at last seen place.	Abandon of *goal* in favor of *playing* with *means.* First ritualizations.	a) Accommodation to new models. b) Imitation of actions of child's repertory, even if child cannot see or hear own actions. c) Imitation by movements that are structurally analogous (ex. opening and closing mouth to imitate eyes).

TABLE 1. (Continued)

	Sensorimotor intelligence	Object	Play: more assimilation than accommodation	Imitation: more accommodation than assimilation
Stage V (12-18 months)	Tertiary circular reactions and discovery of new means by active experimentation. "Experiment in order to see" = pursuit of novelty. Groping behavior directed towards goal.	Object searched for where last seen. But if displacement has to be inferred, child searches under first screen.	Frequent ritualization but only if stimuli are adequate to the schema they evoke.	Imitative behavior becomes more deliberate, active, more precisely accommodated to model.
Stage VI (18 months on)	Invention of new means through mental combination. Invention by "internal trial", by "sensorimotor deduction".	Achievement of object concept: a) object is entity which exists and moves in space. b) permanence of object is independent of child's activity. c) child is one object among others.	True pretense and make-believe by symbolization. Stimuli no longer need to be adequate.	a) Imitation of complex models without groping. b) Imitation of objects and not only of persons. c) Deferred imitation.

3. The child has difficulty in realizing that an object can possess more than one property and thus can belong to several classes at the same time. A long red pencil can belong to the class of pencils, to the class of red objects, to the class of long objects, to the class of writing tools, etc., and one can live in Chicago and in Illinois at the same time. This property of a class is referred to as *multiplicative* classification, or sometimes, more simply, as multiple classification.

Thinking becomes more logical with the emergence of mental operations. Instead of making a judgment about things on the basis of perception, the child begins to *operate* upon the data, to do something with them in his mind. For example, in one of the Piaget tasks, the child is shown a "tower," a long rectangular block of wood, and a number of blocks of the same width, but shorter in height. The "tower" is placed on the floor, and the child is asked to construct another tower, out of the shorter blocks, that will be just as tall as the first one. The experimenter demonstrates with his hands what "just as tall" or "just as long" means. However, the new tower is to be constructed on a low bench rather than on the floor. A four-year-old will build with the shorter blocks until he reaches approximately the same height as the original and then stop. Sometimes he'll take his hand and move it from the top of the first tower through the air to the top of the second to "prove" that both are the same length. He is misled by what he sees—that the two towers have reached the same altitude—and fails to take into account the fact that each starts from a different base. Given a few years time, he will stop making a perceptual judgment centering on the altitude of the two towers; he will be able to reason that he must compensate for the lower base of the original tower by building the second tower higher, and by a precise amount. He begins to realize that the tall block is made up of a number of units of a certain length, and that a tower identical in length may be composed of different units, but they must add up to the same total.

By about seven years of age, logical operations that enable the child to solve problems, like the "tower" problem described above, begin to emerge. This stage of development (roughly from 7 to 11 years) is the *stage of concrete operations;* the child "operates" or transforms mentally the data available to him in a very concrete way. He is not yet able to think about problems in a formal, abstract way, but he does reason logically in a concrete fashion. A very significant mental operation to emerge at this stage is *reversibility;* the mind can reverse an operation, going back to the starting point and comparing it with the present state. For example, suppose the child is given a box of miniature figures—dwellings, human beings, animals, cooking utensils, and miscellaneous objects,—and asked to sort the objects into groups (classes), putting objects alike in some way in the same group. He first thinks, "Some of these are for cooking. I'll put the pot in that pile." Then when he picks up the teakettle or plate, he must go back in thought to what he started with, and ask himself, "Is this for cooking? If so, it goes in the same pile." The child may carry on this operation without thinking in words, but the ability to reverse thinking processes is essential to the successful completion of the task.

Solution of the "tower" problem depends upon other logical operations. One of these is the ability to put together parts to compose a whole, and to realize that the parts can be put together, or associated with one another, in many different ways to add up to the whole. There used to be a colloquial expression, "It doesn't matter how you slice it; it's still baloney" which illustrates the logical truth of the property of *associativity*, or putting parts together in different ways to compose the whole. But *all* the parts must be included to make up the whole. We sometimes remind the child or the adult with whom we are arguing about an important fact that he has omitted in stating his case, a fact which may change the whole case if it is logically inconsistent with the rest of his argument. The *whole* truth is essential in thinking logically as well as in trying cases in a courtroom.

Being able to establish whether things are the same or not, and being able to do something to maintain the identity of an object are other important mental operations to emerge in the stage of concrete operations. We can put two balls of clay on a two-pan balance to see if they weigh the same. If they do not, we can add to the lighter one or take a piece off the heavy one. Then we can take one of the balls off the scale, roll it out into a long hot dog, and put it back on the scale, predicting in advance that the weight will be the same. If nothing is added and nothing is taken away, things remain the same. This logical truth is recognized and, indeed, enunciated by children who are thinking operationally.

The task of the preschool is to provide the foundation for the emergence of logical operations. These do not emerge on the basis of chronological age alone. In fact, there are children of eight and nine years who still think pre-operationally; they are considerably handicapped in school learning, for much of what the school has to teach depends upon the ability to think logically and consistently. Piaget has this to say about the *stage-age* relationship:

> The age of seven is a relative one in a double sense. In our research we say that a problem is solved by children of a certain age when three-quarters of the children of this age respond correctly. As a result, to say that a question is solved at seven years old means that already one-half of the six-year-olds can solve it, and a third of the five-year-olds, etc. So, it's essentially relative to a statistical convention. Secondly, it's relative to the society in which one is working. We did our work in Geneva and the ages that I quote are the ages we found there. I know that in certain societies, for instance in Martinique, where our experiments have been done by Monique Laurendeau and Father Pinard, we have found a systematic delay of three or four years. Consequently the age at which those problems are solved is also relative to the society in question. What is important about these stages is the order of the succession. The mean chronological age is variable. (Ripple and Rockcastle, 1964, pp. 31-32.)

The children in Martinique whom Piaget mentions are poor children, culturally and educationally deprived. The compensatory educational programs in this country are aimed at helping such children catch up. *When* to help these children is no longer controversial (except, perhaps, the precise age); there is general agreement that the period of early childhood is the time when proper intervention will have its maximum impact upon the development of intelligence. *How* to help these children is still being debated, but there is general agreement on one point—that it is important to plan a curriculum that will *sharpen the intelligence of children.* In the long run, a sharpened intelligence will enable a child to participate more successfully in school than will the mastery of a particular skill, like reading.

Dr. Magoun (1960) has pointed out that the evolution of man's brain is probably finished; that there have been no significant changes in the cerebral cortex of *homo sapiens* in the last 45,000 years, and that we will have to look for increased intellectual power to individual post-natal development. Modern man must substitute for phylogenetic changes (changes that come about in the course of man's evolutionary history) maturational changes in the brain acquired as a result of experiences after birth. The quality of early experiences should therefore be of primary concern to educators. And we need to be concerned about the early experiences of *all* children—the immigrant worker's child, the Puerto Rican, the Mexican, the Negro, the lower-class as well as the middle-and upper-class child. Unless each and every child is provided with a good start during his formative years, he may end up at age 40 a permanently unemployed person. An automated America needs fewer and fewer workers with underdeveloped brains.

PIAGET'S EQUILIBRATION MODEL

To foster the growth of intelligence, then, should be one of the goals of preschool education. Piaget's research and writings have provided us with sound theoretical insight into how this goal might be accomplished. His equilibration model describes what goes on in the acquisition of knowledge and, incidentally, in the development of logical intelligence. For Piaget, logical thinking develops as we use our heads to acquire knowledge, and in order to acquire knowledge, we need to have available to us certain logical ways of thinking. Basic to the acquisition is self-activity; acquisition of knowledge is something that "the pupil has to do himself and for himself." It is the nature of the self-activity that Piaget describes for us.

Piaget was a biologist before becoming a psychologist and epistemologist, and so it is not hard to understand that his conception of intelligence is couched in a biological framework, as a basic tendency toward equilibrium in mental structures. There is such a basic homeostatic tendency in other systems of the body; when there is a disturbance to any system, various mechanisms go to work automatically to restore equilibrium to that system. If, for example, the body becomes overheated, automatic mechanisms act to induce sweating, dilate blood vessels and carry on other bodily changes that will lower temperature and restore temperature equilibrium. These are biological adaptations.

Piaget finds adaptation in mental processes as well, but of a superior form. When equilibrium in mental structures is upset, there is a basic tendency to restore it. However, in this case, adjustment is not automatic; the individual exercises some control over the operations of intelligence. Furthermore, mental structures are actually changed by the equilibration process.

Two mechanisms are important in equilibration: *assimilation* and *accommodation*. There is assimilation each time that an individual incorporates into his own mental framework the data from an experience. However, to assimilate an object or a situation, one must act upon it and transform it in some way. New objects or events then become incorporated in intelligence as a scheme or concept that can be repeated and applied in different situations.

Piaget (1952b) distinguishes three types of assimilation: reproductive assimilation, where one reproduces an action in cognitive activity; recognitive assimilation, by which one screens objects that can be assimilated into a particular scheme; and generative assimilation, which permits the enlargement of a scheme to encompass a wider range of objects or events to be assimilated. The reader may recognize these three types in his own mental activity.

The simplest form, recognitive assimilation, is to repeat an idea to oneself; for example, one might say: "Piaget says that self-activity of a mental nature is essential to the act of knowing." In the second form, one might say, "If I simply repeat the idea from memory without 'thinking' about it, without trying to understand what Piaget says about the necessity for self-activity, can I really 'know' what Piaget is talking about?" Here, one is screening a particular idea to see if it will fit a particular scheme. Assimilation of a generative sort is what one does when one says, "What I am doing now is carrying on mental activity in order to understand what Piaget means by self-activity. I'm really acting upon and extending the idea." In other words, one is enlarging the scheme to be assimilated. In each case, the reader is doing something with the data, though his thought processes become more complex as he goes from simple, reproductive assimilation to a higher type.

The transformation of data by the subject finds its counterpart in modification of the exciting framework of thought. This modification is accomplished through the process of accommodation. Accommodation consists of refining and modifying the framework so as to incorporate the data one has assimilated. In accommodation, one "makes up one's mind" about what one believes or accepts as true. The changes in framework are not submitted to passively by the subject; like assimilation, accommodation is an active and an orienting process. There is no accommodation, no change in the framework of thought if the learner is content to state merely the inadequacy of the existing framework; he must take a stand, or make up his mind, about the new data.

Accommodation presupposes effort and initiative on the part of the learner; he must make a "choice," as Piaget puts it. To take a classroom example, let us suppose that the learner is exposed to data that challenge some previously held notion. He may see a demonstration or carry on an experiment in which he finds that a cylinder of lead will raise the level of water in a glass to exactly the same height as a cylinder of aluminum of equal volume. His previously held notion was that the heavier cylinder would raise the water level higher. What does he do with the data that he has assimilated? He can think, "Oh, there's something queer going on, but I'm not going to bother about it," or he can think, "Maybe there's something funny about these two particular cylinders. I'll try two others the same over-all size, one heavy and one light, and see what happens." He may continue his experimentation, varying volume of cylinders next, and assimilating data from each experiment until he convinces himself that some factor other than weight is the cause of the phenomenon he is witnessing. He must take a stand, "It's not weight; it must be something else," and with continued assimilation from his next experiments, he may eventually discover that cylinders of equal volume will displace equal amounts of water, regardless of their weight.

Through progressive assimilations and accommodations, equilibration proceeds and equilibrium is achieved at a higher level. Equilibrium is not a static state; it is, rather, a dynamic compensation resulting from activity of the subject in response to exterior disturbances at a given point in time. Piaget (1964) speaks of a stable state in an open system; the state does not attain a final form but continues to change as new factors enter the system, leading to successive refinements both in knowledge and in the instruments of thought.

Bruner's (1964) discussion of the importance of self-activity sheds additional light on the problem. He sees the child, as he carries on an activity or experiment, building inside himself a mental image of the process. Bruner reports on an experiment in which he attempted to teach children quadratic functions in such a way that children would be able to use their knowledge in the solution of problems. In the first task, children were to lay out cubic blocks in different ways and to see how many ways would be possible for a given number of blocks. From their activity, the children grasped the notion of factoring—that three rows of three cubes made nine, that three such layers had the dimensions of 3″ x 3″ x 3″. Later, a balance beam was introduced, with the task to discover the different combinations of rings that could be put on one side of the balance beam to balance a single ring placed on the opposite side.

Additional activities with building materials were also carried on, in which the child marked off squares on a large flat square with strips of wood and little squares. He was asked, in each case, to record how long and how wide the square was. His first descriptions are very concrete: an X-square (X, the child is told, is an unknown), two X-strips, and a one square. He can check each written description by going back to his construction. As Bruner puts it (p. 326), "The syntactical insights . . . are matched by perceptual-manipulated insights about the material referents."

Obviously, the child should not continue to lean on visible, manipulable materials; he must be able to deal with abstractions or symbols. Given direct, physical experiences, he will assimilate enough data to build a mental representation of the essence of those experiences. A variety of ways of dealing with the concept would seem to be called for. Only one experience with twirling an object on the end of a string may not free the child from the restricting influence of a single sensorimotor act, but a number of activities in which the child "feels" the outward pull of a projectile will enable him to develop a preferred way of thinking about projectile problems. He will not rely upon one image based upon one act, but will have built an image that has abstracted the properties of many acts.

There is no empirical evidence collected in carefully controlled research to prove that acquisition of knowledge depends upon self-activity operating according to an equilibration model. Teachers can find evidence of the dependency, however, in the behavior of their pupils. It is not unusual to find a child completely unconvinced of a principle that he has seen demonstrated or heard explained. Indeed, a teacher may exclaim in irritation at a pupil who gives the wrong answer, "But you've just heard the opposite. We've just gone over the explanation. Weren't you listening?" Privately, the teacher may think the child either stupid or stubborn, but more likely the child has not acted upon the explanation to make it his own, and so equilibration has not occurred.

INDIVIDUAL DIFFERENCES IN RATE OF KNOWLEDGE ACQUISITION

For Piaget, equilibration is the key factor in explaining why some children advance more quickly in the development of logical intelligence than do others. He does not discount such factors as maturation, but he does not find them sufficient. He points out that we cannot anticipate that children, by virtue of having reached a certain age, will have reached a certain state in logical development. The Martinique children, retarded by four years over Geneva norms, are a case in point. More than a neural ripening is essential to the emergence of logical operations. Nor is exposure to a particular experience enough. Deutsch found migratory workers' children, who had crossed the country many times as their parents followed the crops, whose knowledge of the geography of the region was minimal. Nor does instruction which depends upon verbal transmission apparently guarantee emergence of logical structures; readers have probably had the experience of listening to or reading about a clear account of the scientific discovery of a Nobel prize winner and of feeling that they understood the explanation, only to find it totally impossible to explain the phenomenon to others.

Self-activity is crucial to the equilibration model. If equilibration is to be achieved at a higher level, then the child must be mentally active. *He* must transform the data. The elements to be incorporated may be present in an experience, or the child may be told of the error in his thinking, but unless the mind is actively engaged in wrestling with data, no accommodation, or false accommodation, occurs. Children, like adults, are not convinced by being told that they are wrong. They have to act upon the data and transform them. As Piaget puts it, knowledge is not a copy of reality; to know something one must modify reality.

Piagetian theory also makes it clear that perceptual processes and operational processes are two quite different forms of mental activity, and that training perceptual skills will not lead to the transformation of data essential to logical thinking. Tasks where pupils sort colors and shapes can be performed at the perceptual level. A child can form a class of red objects without shuffling any data about in his head; he can simply make a perceptual judgment. Piaget has argued convincingly that one does not train for logical thinking by training perception. He points out (1961),

1. Perception is dependent upon the presence of the object, and perceptual knowledge is limited to certain physical characteristics. Perception of a rectangle, for example, is limited to the shape, dimensions and size of the particular rectangle being perceived. Operative structures (intelligence), on the other hand, can evoke the object even in its absence, and in its presence can interpret the rectangle as a particular case of rectangles, or even of quadrilateral figures in general.

2. Perception is bounded by limits of space and time. In viewing a full moon, one can only perceive at the same time its quarter by evoking memory or an operative structure. Intelligence, on the other hand, can consider any element independent of space-time, and can equally as well dissociate neighboring objects and reason about them in complete independence.

3. Perception is essentially egocentric; what is perceived is special to the point of view of a particular person. Furthermore, it is subject to systematic deformations through centration effects (an over-valuation of those elements upon which perception centers). The intelligence of operations, on the other hand, makes possible knowledge of an object apart from self,

and from the particular point of view of an individual. Operational structures enable one to view objects or events from viewpoints other than the narrow, restricted one afforded by the perceptual.

4. Perception is limited to that which is cognizable by the senses. In perceiving a box which is closed, for example, one sees only a box in three dimensions with a particular volume and an interior, but other mechanisms are necessary to decide about the contents of the box. Intelligence, on the other hand, can go beyond sensory data and make a deductive guess about what the box contains.

5. Perceptual structures ignore abstractions; they cannot restrict themselves to certain elements of an object or event while making an abstraction of others. It is the province of intelligence to choose which data are necessary to resolve a particular problem and to pass up other data.

Many preschool programs are presently emphasizing perceptual training as a means of improving learning ability, and particularly ability to learn to read. But if the skill to be learned demands that data be transformed (as reading does), the perceptual training contributes little. Only when the child must, in some way, change what he perceives around him is logical thinking involved.

A PIAGETIAN MODEL FOR EARLY CHILDHOOD EDUCATION

Experimental programs in early childhood education have tended to set as their goal the raising of the IQ. As one psychologist has facetiously put it, "American teachers seem to have set as their goal raising the IQ of children so that everyone is above the 50th percentile." A more realistic goal for the preschool would be the development of intellectual competence, recognizing that such factors as motivation and self-concept are involved in intellectual competence. Such a goal contrasts sharply with the goal of curricula like the Bereiter-Engelmann (1966), designed to develop pre-academic skills in reading, language and arithmetic. And, implementation of a goal to develop intellectual competence would mean a day mostly unstructured in contrast to one in the pre-academic preschool where every minute of the child's time is involved in highly structured activity. If we accept Piaget's theory that knowledge is acquired through action upon things and the relations which exist between them, then a major part of the preschool day should be reserved for free choice of activity. The activity may be carried on individually, or it may involve other children. We should not lose sight of the fact that children teach one another, and a program which restricts choice of activity deprives children of the opportunity to learn from each other.

But, as we have pointed out earlier, *some* children make exciting discoveries as they carry on transactions in the preschool; others do not. *Some*, like the child Montessori observed, performing an activity over 40 times, will stay with an activity for long periods of time; others will flit from one activity to another. *Some* will carry on "directed experimentation" in their play with materials; others will use materials only to manipulate for sensorimotor satisfaction.

How to help *all* children acquire knowledge through self-activity is the teacher's task. Teachers in some of the British Infant Schools appear to be able to do this through adroit questioning of the children as they explore a piece of equipment. One American observer commented upon the fact that the British teacher appeared to be able to ask exactly the right question at the right time, so that children were motivated to carry on their activity at a higher level. For example, to a child who was sorting geometric shapes of two different sizes and colors and making many piles of the shapes, the teacher said, "How can you sort them so that you have only two piles and still use all the shapes?" The teacher in such instances does not tell the child what to do, but her questions may pose a problem for the child to solve, the solution to which may result in reaching equilibrium in mental processes at a higher level.

But how can a teacher know what questions to ask? One way is to be aware of cognitive developments during the early childhood years, and here Piagetian theory is invaluable. The preschool child is likely to be at a pre-operational stage of thinking processes, and we know how the child is thinking about his world during this stage. We know that he is sorting out what he sees and beginning to form classes and subclasses. We know that he is developing notions of space and number, and of how the two are related. We know that he is beginning to order things and events, to arrange them in a series from small to large, short to tall, first to last or light to heavy. We know what the important cognitive developments are for most children, and we can plan a curriculum based upon these developments. In particular, we can plan a curriculum centered on classification, space and number, and seriation (ordering) based upon our knowledge of step-by-step development in these areas. And as the child engages in activities in these areas, he will be assimilating new knowledge and changing old ideas, with the result that his thinking will become more logical.

An outline of logical processes as they appear developmentally in early childhood in each of the three areas—Classification (Inhelder and Piaget, 1964), Space and Number (Piaget, 1952a; Piaget and Inhelder, 1956; Piaget, Inhelder and Szeminska, 1960), Seriation (Inhelder and Piaget, 1964) — follows:

CLASSIFICATION:

1. *Simple Sorting.* The child groups objects according to a single property perceptually apparent, like color, size or shape.

2. *Emergence of True Classification.* Abstracting the common property in a group of objects and finding that same property in other objects in the group. The child is able to carry on both of these processes simultaneously.

3. *Multiplicative Classification.* The child can classify by more than one property at a time and can recognize that an object can belong to several classes at the same time.

4. *All-Some Relation.* The child can distinguish classes on the basis of a property belonging to *all* members of the class and a property belonging to *some* members of the class. In a display of red squares and red circles, for example, he recognizes that *all* the shapes are red, and that only *some* are square and *some* are circles.

5. *Class-Inclusion Relation.* The child can form subclasses of objects (a class of red beads and a class of yellow beads) and can include the subclasses in a larger class (the class of wooden beads).

SPACE AND NUMBER:

1. *Physical Correspondence of Objects on a One-to-One Basis.* The child can establish equality between two sets of objects when the objects correspond visually.

2. *One-to-One Correspondence When Physical Correspondence is Destroyed.* The child recognizes equality between sets of objects even in the absence of spatial equivalence.

3. *Conservation of Quantity.* The child recognizes that a particular quantity, whether it is a liquid quantity, like water, or a quantity of discrete objects, like beads, does not vary when the quantity is moved so that it occupies a different space. Ten is ten regardless of whether the 10 objects are in a low flat container or a tall thin one, spread out in space or bunched together.

4. *Conserving the Whole When the Additive Composition of its Parts is Varied.* The child understands that 8 objects divided into sets of 4 and 4 are numerically equivalent to 8 objects distributed 1 and 7.

5. *Conservation of Area.* The child recognizes that area is conserved even though its appearance may change, provided nothing is added or taken away.

6. *Transformation of Perspective.* The child is able to picture how an object would look when viewed from a different vantage point, or to turn things around in his mind in order to visualize how they would look after a transformation in space.

SERIATION:

1. *Ordering Objects in a Series According to One Property.* The child is able to put objects in order from shortest to tallest (or some other property), and to include *all* the objects to be ordered.

2. *Ordering Objects in Two Series Inversely Related to One Another.* The child is able to think of two relations at once, and to reverse the order of arrangement from shortest to tallest or thinnest to fattest.

3. *Seriation and Visual Representation.* The child is able to draw a picture of objects he has arranged in a series and, later, to draw the picture in advance of arranging.

4. *Seriation of Geometric Shapes.* The child can order a set of geometric shapes increasing in area and number of sides.

All preschool curricula include some classification, number and space and seriating activities, but not all teachers are aware of the separate thought processes involved in each area, or of the order in which these processes emerge in the developmental timetable. Awareness of how structures grow will provide guidelines for the teachers in choosing materials and in knowing what to say to children as they use the materials. Descriptions of structures and how they develop in each of these three areas—classification, number and space, seriation—are presented in detail in Chapters 4, 5 and 6, together with suggested activities for fostering such developments.

Short, structured periods are helpful in developing teacher sophistication of how structures develop and how to aid such development. The teacher may set aside a period of ten or fifteen minutes a day in which a small group of five or six children will work intensively with her, or with an assistant, on, say, problems of one-to-one correspondence. During this period, the teacher directs the children's activity and questions them about what they are doing and why they are doing it. In this way, she finds out how children are thinking about the problem.

The "clinical interview" used in Geneva in testing children on Piagetian tasks serves as a helpful model. In the clinical interview, the experimenter first presents the stimulus to the child, then transforms the stimulus in some way, asks the child questions about the transformation and, finally, asks the child to justify his answers. Included in Appendix 2 are directions for such interviews.

The teacher can adapt the clinical interview for her work with small groups of children. Each child can be provided with materials upon which he operates according to the teacher's directions. For example, he may be asked to sort flowers into two groups: daisies and flowers other than daisies, or to line up from a collection of pennies as many as needed to buy 10 miniature cars laid out in a row, or to arrange a collection of flowers-in-pots from smallest to largest. In each case, the child is called upon to explain what he is doing and why.

When the child makes a mistake, the teacher does not *tell* him he is wrong or tell him how to correct what he has done. As Piaget has pointed out, telling is not teaching and is not convincing. The *child* must transform the data, by reversing his action, or putting parts together in different ways, or by some other logical means. The teacher can suggest such ways of operating upon the materials in order to facilitate the transformational process. For example, in a one-to-one activity, the teacher can ask the child to line up the materials as they were originally, or to add one item to one of the rows, or to take one away, and in each case, to compare rows by establishing physical correspondence.

The concept of readiness is important here. Readiness depends upon the child's existing state of knowledge. Some things must be learned before others; more difficult concepts are built upon a foundation of simpler ones, and the teacher must be sure that the proper foundation has been laid for whatever she is going to teach. In the case of one-to-one correspondence, physical or visual correspondence precedes conservation of number when visual correspondence is destroyed. If the child does not see that the number of objects is conserved or remains the same, even after a transformation in the amount of space the objects occupy, the teacher can suggest things to do to the materials to help develop the concept. And, if the notion of physical correspondence is lacking, if the child does not see that he must lay out one penny for one car and must do this for every car, then the teacher may suggest a simpler activity, like having the child drop a bean from each hand into separate containers of different shapes, and then questioning him about equality of number.

Piaget has pointed out that administering Piagetian tasks and listening to children's responses will help the teacher become more aware of thinking processes; so will carrying out directed activities as just suggested. And with her increasing sophistication, the teacher will be better prepared to ask the adroit question or suggest a new line of inquiry to individual children during their periods of self-chosen, self-directed, activity. No daily ten-minute period of mental gymnastics is going to work miracles in developing intellectual competence, but when the teacher knows how to reinforce the learnings of the directed periods *throughout the day*, as children paint, set tables, build with blocks, play house, etc., she increases the likelihood that generalization of the concept will occur and that transfer of training will be possible.

The use of special materials in the structured periods may suggest to the teacher additional materials to provide for unstructured periods. Building blocks, clay, paints, housekeeping equipment—all are basic equipment of early childhood classrooms; but needed also are a variety of materials for concept building. Classifying, conserving, seriating concepts are more likely to be acquired from experiences with many different kinds of materials.

How to put such a curriculum into action? The following is a summary of implications of Piagetian theory:

1. Intelligence grows through the twin processes of assimilation and accommodation. In the process of assimilation, the child incorporates new elements from his experiences into existing structures; in the process of accommodation, existing structures change to accommodate to the new inputs. Experiences should be planned to allow opportunities for assimilation and accommodation.

2. Activity of the learner is essential. It is only as the child is forced to go beyond perceptual decisions to act mentally on what he is assimilating that mental structures change and intelligence grows. *Activity* as used here is *mental* activity, but, at the preschool level, exploration and manipulation of concrete materials are needed to stimulate mental activity.

3. As the child explores and manipulates, he makes discoveries. Some of his discoveries are wrong, but over a period of time he assimilates enough data from his experience to make corrections. Whenever possible, feedback should be provided so that the child can figure out whether or not he is on the right track. For example, if the child has the task of setting a table with knife, fork, and spoon in the same position relative to the hand on opposite sides of the table, he can move from one side of the table to the other to see if he has made the transformation correctly.

4. The teacher's role is to stimulate and guide, not to teach specific responses, not to tell the child the right answer, nor even to tell him that he is wrong. The teacher must have confidence in the child's ability to learn *on his own.* When he is wrong, she may ask questions or call attention to cues that he has missed so that he has more data to assimilate, but giving him the right answer will not convince the child. *He* must be convinced by *his own* actions.

A number of schools in the United States are presently following a Piaget-type curriculum, and there are some data available as to its effectiveness. A midwestern suburban community put such a curriculum into effect in its public school kindergartens. Children enrolled in the schools were from low to upper socio-economic-status families, with the bulk of families being middle-class. IQ's (Binet) ranged from 82 to 144.

Sixteen kindergartens participated in the program; 50 children were selected at random from the total kindergarten population as an experimental group. They were matched for IQ S.E.S. (Socio-Economic-Status), sex and C.A. (Chronological Age) with 50 controls in another community.

TABLE 2.   SIGNIFICANCE OF THE DIFFERENCES
IN MEAN SCORES BETWEEN THE EXPERIMENTAL
AND CONTROL GROUPS*

Test	Experi-mental Group Mean	Control Group Mean	Mean Differ-ence	Signif-icance
Conservation of Matter	3.14	2.77	0.37	N.S.**
Conservation of Length	2.88	2.00	0.88	.01
Conservation of Surface	1.88	1.80	0.08	N.S.**
Seriation	2.41	1.86	0.55	.01
Composite	10.31	8.43	1.88	.05

In the experimental classrooms, the teacher began by introducing each activity to a group of six students at a time. For example, she presented a matrix puzzle and had the children work on it as a group so that each child understood how the material was to be used. Then the matrix puzzles were left on open shelves for the children to use during their free play periods. An answer card was prepared and inserted in the same envelope with each puzzle so that the child might check his responses when he finished.

* From a report prepared by James M. Dunlap, Coordinator Research and Testing, School District of University City, University City, Missouri, March, 1966.
** N.S. — Not Significant.

Additional ways of using the equipment, calling forth progressively more difficult logical processes were introduced, again in structured lessons to a small group of students, as children mastered the first step. (In some instances, progressive difficulty was built into the materials, as with the matrix puzzles, for example.) The structured sessions also gave the teacher an opportunity to assess the progress of the children and to alert them to cues they might be overlooking. All children participated in two such structured small-group sessions each week during a five-month period.

At the end of five months of these formal-informal procedures, five Piaget tasks were presented to children in both experimental and control groups. Tasks were selected that would test for transfer of logical skills, tasks sufficiently different from the activities the children had been engaged in so that the children could not be said to have been trained for the tasks.

As can be seen in Table 2, results on all five tests favored the experimental group and results on three of the tests were significant at the .01 level.

For maximum effectiveness, training for language competence can be combined with training logical intelligence. It is possible to use language in the small-group sessions in such a way that the children's abilty to communicate effectively with others is strengthened. Furthermore, there is a relationship between thought and language; clear thinking is essential to a clear expression of ideas, but language, in turn, can help to clarify fuzzy thought. It is the relationship between thought and language that we consider in the next chapter and what kind of language training might be combined with training to foster logical thinking.

Herb Weitman, University City Public Schools, University City, Missouri

Children at the Prekindergarten Research Center, University City, Missouri, work on a spatial transformation problem. Given a man in a park with a road, stream, hills, trees and houses, where will that man be located in an identical park that has been turned around by 180°? Adults often find it difficult to make such a transformation in the mind because of lack of training in visualizing an object in space. Training sessions to foster development of such skills also involve considerable language training. Terms such as *on one side, on the other side, in back of, in front of, lower than, higher than,* take on meaning when taught in connection with concrete experiences.

3. Training for Language and Intellectual Competence*

A NOTED AUTHORITY on the study of language has said, "The ability to learn language is so deeply rooted in man that children learn it even in the face of dramatic handicaps." The grammar that they acquire may not be the "King's English," but even children from impoverished disorganized homes know and use all parts of speech by the time they enter kindergarten. Their very mistakes reveal that they have acquired the rules. When a child says "footses" for "feet," he is revealing a knowledge of one of our rules for forming plurals; he is simply not aware of all the exceptions.

But despite the child's natural capacity for language and his remarkable progress in this area in a few years' time, children do need help in making words do what they want them to do—namely, to express ideas clearly. We ask, then, what should be the place of language training in the preschool curriculum and, especially, in a curriculum designed to foster logical thinking? Does the ability to use language competently contribute to clear thinking, or does clear thinking precede the clear expression of ideas? Can we make children better thinkers by training them in the language pro-

* A shorter version of this chapter appeared as a paper entitled "An Approach to Language Learning," and is reprinted here with permission from *Young Children*, Vol. XXIV, No. 6, Sept., 1969. National Association for the Education of Young Children, 1834 Connecticut Avenue, N.W., Washington, D.C.

cesses? These are questions on which psychologists and educators are divided.

For Piaget, language is a symptom of underlying thought. That is, it is the kind of logic that the child is capable of that gets expressed in words. Thus, as Piaget studied empirically the development of language processes in the young child, he found reflected there evidence of the same characteristics described as pre-operational thinking.

Piaget's (1967) recent work on the development of causality is interesting in this connection. He describes three stages in the young child's thinking about causality. In the first stage, explanations tend to be *finalistic;* that is, the child finds purpose in natural events. Asked why water flows downhill, he says, "because it has to go into the lake." In the second stage, explanations are characterized by *dynamism;* the child attributes a kind of animate power to water, and the water flows downhill "because it has movement." Later, in the third stage, the child gives *mechanistic* explanations; water flows downhill "because it is heavy" or "because of gravity." Note that the word "because" appears in all three explanations. The use of the word does not denote that the child in this case has an accurate notion of causality; he uses "because" in a very loose way to denote a relationship between ideas which may or may not be causal.

If we follow Piaget's train of thought to its logical conclusion, then one would assume that the verbal expression of ideas would become clearer only as ideas become more logical. Yet thought and language *do* appear to interact with one another. In searching for the right words to express our ideas, we often find that the ideas lose some of their fuzziness and become clearer and more logical. That is why teaching a difficult concept to others often helps to clarify it in our own minds. We are forced to operate upon our ideas, ironing out inconsistencies, so that we can communicate more clearly. As Vygotsky put it, thought and language are interrelated; language is "the handmaiden of thought," but thought also serves language. Can the conflict between these two points of view be resolved and the resolution applied to language training?

In recent years, the whole issue of language training has assumed tremendous importance in early education programs, for language is the vehicle of school instruction and the child who does not have adequate possession of language is handicapped in school learning. The lower-class child, in particular, is handicapped; standardized tests of school achievement show that scores on such tests are correlated with socio-economic status; the lower the class, the greater the number of students who score below grade. Particularly in reading is the disability marked; disadvantaged seventh and eighth graders who test at the third grade level are not uncommon. Such low scores have been attributed to many factors: little desire to succeed in school, lack of readiness for school learning, poor teaching, and, most frequently, language disability. Can language training be combined with training for logical intelligence so as to overcome the deficit? First, we must examine the nature of the deficit.

THE NATURE OF THE LANGUAGE DEFICIT

What aspect of the lower-class child's language deficit affects his school achievement is still a matter of study. It is generally agreed that the disadvantaged child has a smaller vocabulary than does his middle-class peer, and that he uses substandard English. But whether vocabulary size or use of substandard English affects school learning is debatable. Not knowing five synonyms for "beautiful" and saying "He done it" are unlikely to impede school learning. Nor is there agreement on whether or not a substandard dialect is a hindrance to school learning. A rather generally accepted assumption has been that dialectal differences, both those involving pronunciation and those involving syntax, can contribute to difficulties in learning to read. The prediction is that the child who says, "Did you get 'Ref' (Ralph) to come down to 'hip' (help) you?" may have trouble in recognizing certain regularities in pronunciation when the "l" sound appears in a position other than in the middle of a word. Even greater will be the difficulties of the child whose syntax is radically different from the standard English of textbooks. The child who says, "Dat mine," may find that the wording in his primer, "That is mine," conveys little meaning to him.

At least one investigator (De Boeuf, 1969) has been trying to find out which, if any, deviations in pronunciation affect reading. One hypothesis is that only when the meaning is changed do the deviations make a difference. Often in dialect, final consonants are either dropped or simplified. Where the final consonant is an inflection, the meaning is changed if the consonant is changed or dropped. "I talk to him" means something different from "I talked to him." On the other hand, some deviations may not involve a change in meaning. The "have" in some dialects may be pronounced so that it is almost indistinguishable from "hair" or "hand," but it may be that the words constitute a set of homonyms which would present no more difficulties to the child than "son" or "sun" do to the rest of us. Homonyms take on their unique meaning from the context and, given the word "son" out of context, no one would know whether "son" or "sun" was intended.

Actually we do not know whether children who speak a lower-class dialect have merely a different set of homonyms or whether they have a greater set. If the set is greater, then pronunciation may constitute an additional burden to the child who speaks a dialect. Preschools, at the present time, are expending enormous effort trying to eliminate dialectal differences in pronunciation on the grounds that the children will then be better prepared for reading in the first grade. We need more evidence on this particular point, so that we can focus in intervention programs on the things that really count.

One problem arises because of social attitudes toward a dialect employing substandard grammars. That there is a social class prejudice against such dialects is obvious, and this prejudice is often stated as a reason for changing dialectal grammars to make them conform to standard English. The argument is advanced that if a person is going to participate in the fullest possible sense in American society, he must be able to speak standard English. Occasionally, the Twiggies speaking Cockney English receive wide acceptance, but most Elizas must be able to drop their dialect to move into the middle-class, either black or white. Sometimes, the change in language habits brings rejection by the primary group and, as a result, change is resisted; observers report that some black adolescents refuse to learn standard English because they do not want to talk like Whitey.

While there is agreement over the social problem arising from dialectal differences, there is little agreement over the question of whether or not dialects employing a substandard grammar are a hindrance to thinking processes. The assumption is generally held that such a dialect is a simpler form of language and therefore is less useful as a tool of thought. Psycholinguists, however, dispute this assumption. Klima, in a paper on "Inter-Relatedness of Grammatical Systems," analyzed literary English, the spoken English of Churchill, and two dialectal variations, in terms of the kinds of rules that account for the particular grammatical systems being employed. He showed that it is not the case that one is simpler than another, but simply that there are different ordering rules. In some dialects in this country there is a distinction made between "He sick" or "He tire," which refer to the immediate present, and "He be sick," or "He be tired" which means that he is chronically ill or tired all the time. It is obvious that such distinctions are as difficult to learn as "He's sick," and, "He's busy all the time," and that the rules governing the one case are not inferior to or less demanding than the standard form.

Most European countries have regional dialects differing both in pronunciation and grammar from the standard dialect. Children in such countries learn the standard language in school but continue to use a dialect outside, and no one expresses great concern over the matter. Furthermore, there are no learning deficits resulting from use of the dialect reported.

The whole area of dialectal differences still contains a number of unsolved problems. While reservations are being expressed about whether or not such differences contribute to a cognitive deficit, there still remains the question of whether disadvantaged children speaking a dialect are exposed to a language environment rich enough so that they can make normal progress *in the dialect.* There is also the question of communication and whether a dialect understood adequately only by a minority can ever be an effective vehicle for communication.

Many experts think that while children may retain their dialect for use at home and with peers, children should also have standard English available to them. Schools need not take drastic measures to stamp out the dialect, but they can take steps to see that children make steady progress in the growth of standard English. There is a growing conviction that what is more likely to interfere with school learning than a dialect is the disadvantaged child's inability to use language to meet the demands of the school. When he is asked to follow directions, participate in discussion, compare two objects or events and make discriminations between them, classify or draw inferences, he is often at a loss to do so. In a word, he does not know how to use language to meet cognitive demands.

A number of writers have theorized about the antecedents of this specific disability. From an early study by Milner (1951) came the thesis that patterns of family life, including opportunity for two-way conversations in the family, might account for differences. She investigated two groups of Negro children, high and low scorers on the language criteria of the California Test of Mental Maturity. She studied the patterns of parent-child interaction and found striking differences between the two groups. Families of high scorers had meals together and engaged in two-way conversation at the meals. Such two-way conversations were lacking in the families of low-scorers. Differences described by Milner are usually associated with socio-economic differences. Lower-class disorganized families are more likely to be characterized by the patterns of family living Milner found among low-scorers on readiness tests.

Bernstein (1961), in several provocative papers, noted that lower-class parents tend to use a "restricted" code in talking to their children in contrast to the "elaborated" one used by middle-class parents. In the restricted code, only short, grammatically simple sentences are used, with little use of subordinate clauses, limited use of adjectives and adverbs, frequent instances of illogical statements and few specific referents, with the speaker often taking it for granted that the listener knows what he's talking about. Some of the characteristics of the restricted code are:

1.   Short, grammatically simple, often unfinished sentences with a poor syntactical form stressing the active voice.

2.   Simple and repetitive use of conjunctions (*so, then, because*).

3.   Little use of subordinate clauses to break down the initial categories of the dominant subject.

4.   Inability to hold a formal subject through a speech sequence; thus a dislocated informational content is facilitated.

5. Rigid and limited use of adjectives and adverbs.

6. Infrequent use of impersonal pronouns as subjects of conditional clauses.

7. Frequent use of statements where the reason and conclusion are confounded to produce a categoric statement.

8. A large number of statements/phrases which signal a requirement for the previous speech sequence to be reinforced: "Wouldn't it?" "You see?" "You know?", etc. This process is termed "sympathetic circularity."

9. Individual selection from a group of idiomatic phrases or sequences.

10. Individual qualification implicit in the sentence organization: it is a language of implicit meaning.

Note that these characteristics are indeed likely to create difficulties for the child in meeting the cognitive demands of the school. Note especially items numbered 4, 7, and 10 which involve the clear communication of ideas, and for which special provision should be made in a training program.

Hess and Shipman (1968) studied parent-teaching styles in an effort to describe more precisely how mothers influence language development. Mothers and children, both low and middle class, all Negro, were brought to the laboratory at the University of Chicago Early Education Research Center, where each mother was to teach the same content to her child. The investigators analyzed what went on in the lessons in terms of how well the mothers transmitted information, as well as in terms of other variables. The tasks involved sorting objects into groups and explaining the sorting principles. To be effective, the mother had to be able to communicate specific meanings clearly and precisely. The teaching of many mothers, however, was poorly organized or incomplete. Some mothers simply said, "That's not right," when the child made a mistake, leaving him in the dark as to what to do next. In contrast, some mothers would point to the erroneously placed block and the other block and say, "No, see, this block has an *O* on it and these have *X*. You don't want to mix up the *O*'s and the *X*'s, so you have to put this block where there are some other blocks that have *O* on them, too." Children of such mothers were more successful in completing the task than those whose mothers could not transmit information specifically enough to teach the child what to do.

In addition, successful mothers used praise and encouragement rather than criticism and coercive control to motivate their children. The contrast between the two is shown in the following example:

1a "I've got another game to teach you."

1b "There's another thing you have to learn here, so sit down and pay attention."

2a "Now listen to Mommy carefully and watch what I do because I'm going to show you how we play the game."

2b "Pay attention now and get it right, 'cause you're gonna have to show the lady how to do it later."

3a "No, Johnny. That's a big one. Remember we're going to keep the big ones separate from the little ones."

3b "No, that's not what I showed you! Put that with the big ones where it belongs."

4a "Wait a minute, Johnny. You have to look at the block first before you try to find where it goes. Now pick it up again and look at it—is it big or small? . . . Now put it where it goes."

4b "That doesn't go there— you're just guessing. I'm trying to show you how to do this and you're just putting them any old place. Now pick it up and do it again and this time don't mess up."

5a "No, we can't stop now, Johnny. Mrs. Smith wants me to show you how to do this so you can do it for her. Now if you pay close attention and let Mommy teach you, you can learn how to do it and show her, and then you'll have some time to play."

5b "Now you're playing a-round and you don't even know how to do this. You want me to call the lady? You better listen to what I'm saying and quit playing around or I'm gonna call the lady in on you and see how you like that."

Note that the successful mothers made the task seem desirable, rather than a chore, with the mother in the role of supportive sponsor or helper rather than an impersonal or primitive authority figure. Affective behavior of the mother contributes to her effectiveness as a teacher.

Hess and Shipman found social class differences in the teaching behaviors of the mothers. All mothers in the study were black but were from four different social groups: a college-educated professional, executive and managerial level: a skilled blue-collar level; a semi-skilled level with a predominantly elementary school education; and a lower-level class group on ADC (Aid to Dependent Children). Lower-class mothers, poorly educated, and with the lowest IQ's, were the least effective in teaching their children, while upper-middle-class mothers were most effective. One can safely predict which children are going to be successful school learners. And, while a comparable study has not been made of teacher behavior, one suspects that teachers would differ, too, in their ability to communicate specific meanings clearly and precisely, and to support children's problem-solving attempts.

One additional analysis of the needs of the lower-class child might be mentioned here. Moore (1969) has reviewed the literature on subcultural differences in children's language abilities and finds two major problems that contribute to the learning difficulties of the lower-class child. One is the inability to use a "language of reference" to describe precisely, by use of appropriate modifiers, what the speaker is talking about, the other is the inability to use language in the "abstract" where the objects or events under discussion are not present, and so the bulk of the communication burden falls upon language.

Schools obviously have a remedial job to do in the case of the many lower-class children whose training in the use of the language has been inadequate. But middle-class children also need help. They may speak the "King's English" but still have difficulty in putting thoughts into words, in expressing ideas sequentially, in keeping to the subject in a speech sequence and in stating reasons for actions. They may need help in giving precise descriptions of objects and events and in giving logical explanations of actions or phenomena. The problem is obviously more than one of increasing the child's vocabulary or his grammatical repertoire. It is one of teaching him the language essential for receiving and communicating ideas. And, as we have pointed out, this kind of language is closely tied to thought: we want the child to grow more logical in his thinking and to be able to express his logical thought adequately. Now for a closer look at the question with which we began: the relationship between language and thought, and whether language training can assist the development of logical thinking. To do this, we will begin with a further exposition of the Piagetian position.

THE RELATIONSHIP BETWEEN LOGIC AND LANGUAGE

Two main points that Piaget and Inhelder make with respect to the relationship between logic and language are: (Sinclair, 1969)

1. The *sources* of intellectual operations are not to be found in language but in the actions the child carries on upon objects and events in the environment during the sensorimotor period. Piaget cites the example of an infant searching for a watch chain he has seen placed first under one cushion, then under another and another and, finally, under a fourth. At a particular stage in development, the infant always begins the search under the first pillow where he has seen the chain placed and then proceeds to search under each cushion, in turn, until he finds the chain. Gradually he learns that he can proceed immediately to the proper cushion, without taking the intervening steps. He learns, by carrying out such actions, that there are different paths to the same goal, thus laying the groundwork for development of the logical operation of *associativity* (the parts can associate with one another in different ways). And, by moving the chain from one of the pillows back to the first, he lays the groundwork for development of the logical operation of reversibility. Out of many such actions during the first 18 months of life the groundwork is laid for logical operations. Furthermore, the groundwork is laid during a period when language has barely begun to develop.

2. Language makes its appearance when actions begin to be represented in thought. Thus, representational thought and language are both part of a larger complex of processes having to do with symbolic functions. The child gradually learns to represent reality through the intermediary of symbols or signs; these may be words or mental images or imitations.

Following the sensorimotor period, language development proceeds very rapidly. However, the language of the child, his expression of ideas, becomes clearer, according to Piaget, only as ideas become more logical.

On the other hand, Piaget himself is equivocal on the subject. After stating that language is not causally responsible for basic cognitive development, he then maintains that language may aid in "transforming thought by helping it achieve its forms of equilibrium by a more advanced schematization and a more mobile abstraction." He also notes that while intelligence has its roots in action and in sensorimotor mechanisms, "the more the structures of thought are refined, the more language is necessary for the achievement of this elaboration. Language is thus a necessary but not sufficient condition for the construction of logical operations." And he also states that "classificatory structures are constantly being reinforced by the syntactical structure of language."

Vygotsky (1962) sees a stronger role for language processes in cognitive development. While he theorizes that thought and speech arise independently in the nervous system, he postulates that, when private speech develops, the two systems fuse, and that complex logical thinking depends upon interiorized speech. He was concerned with, "the investigation of how a function, arising in communication and at first divided between two people, can restructure all of the activity of the child and gradually change into the complicated mediated functional system which characterizes the structure of his mental processes." Vygotsky's particular point of view has given rise to considerable research by Russian investigators on the development and function of "inner speech" in children. The approach dates back at least as far as 1863 when Sechenov wrote, "When a child thinks, he invariably talks at the same time. Thought in five-year-olds is mediated through words or whispers . . ." (Slobin, p. 130). Flavell and coworkers (1966) have tested the relationship between inner speech and cognitive functioning and report some success in improving memory following the prompting of private speech.

"Common sense" notions reflect this same point of view regarding inter-relationships between thought and language. Teachers often tell pupils to "think out loud" about a problem they are struggling with, in the belief that, in searching for the right words to express ideas, the ideas lose some of the fuzziness and become clearer and more logical. Then, too, we often hear expressed the advice that if one doesn't understand a concept, one should try to teach it, for expressing it verbally often helps to clarify it. Teaching a concept forces us to operate upon our ideas, ironing out inconsistencies, so that we can communicate more clearly. As Piaget noted (1964), "Nobody knows better than a professor that the best way to learn something is to teach it."

We have already pointed out the importance of being able to use language to meet cognitive demands: that is, to make comparisons, to draw inferences, to see cause-and-effect relationships, to take classes apart and put them together again, to talk about things and events that are not present. Each of these mental operations demands use of a particular syntactical structure for expression. Supplying training on the use of the syntax in an appropriate situation will *not teach* the operation, but *may support* an operation beginning to emerge as the result of self-activities included in a training program to accelerate logical processes. Investigators, such as Wohlwill and Smedslund, have found again and again *not significant* results from using certain training procedures to elicit conservation responses but a *tendency toward* positive results. Could that tendency be strengthened by adding to training procedures, proven partially successful, training for appropriate use of syntactical structures which would support the logical operation being trained for? When we train for classification and seriation operations, will the addition of training on syntactical structures to express the operations yield a significant change in the age of transition? Let us examine the evidence from research for some answers.

Sinclair (1969) has described a series of experiments designed to find out whether young children who differed in their ability to deal with a conservation task would also differ on certain verbal tasks. She found no differences in comprehension tasks; children could understand the statement: "Find a pencil that is *longer* but *thinner.*" However, she did find differences between conservers and non-conservers in the use of comparatives when the children were describing quantity; non-conservers were more likely to use absolute terms like *a lot, a little,* rather than comparative terms, *more than, less than.* Sinclair also found that non-conservers used undifferentiated terms for the two dimensions (one would use *fat* for *long and thick*), and used four separate sentences to describe two objects in two dimensions: "This crayon is *long.* The other is *short.* This crayon is *thin.* The other is *thick.*" Conservers, on the other hand, were able to coordinate the two dimensions in a single sentence, and to use only two sentences to describe both objects: "This pencil is *long* but *thin.* The other is *short* but *thick.*"

Sinclair also reports attempts to teach children without conservation the use of differentiated terms. This task proved easy. She found it harder to teach comparatives (*more, less*), and still harder to teach coordinations (*long and/but thin, short and/but thick*). Her conclusions follow (Sinclair-de-Zwart, 1969, pp. 324-325):

(a) A distinction must be made between lexical acquisition and the acquisition of syntactical structures, the latter being more closely linked to operational level than the former. The operator-like words (e.g., *more, less, as much as, none*) form a class apart whose correct use is also very closely linked to operational progress. The other lexical items (e.g., *long, short, thin, thick, high, low*) are far less closely linked to operativity.

(b) Operational structuring and linguistic structuring, or rather linguistic restructuring, thus parallel each other. The lexical items are already being used or at least easily learned at a pre-operational level; the coordinated structures and operator-like words are correctly "understood" in simple situations, but the latter are precisely and regularly used only with the advent of the first operational structures. Moreover, the difficulties encountered by the child in the use of these expressions seem to be the same as those he encounters in the development of the operations themselves: lack of decentration and incapacity to coordinate.

(c) Verbal training leads subjects without conservation to direct their attention to pertinent aspects of the problem (covariance of the dimensions), but it does not *ipso facto* bring about the acquisition of operations.

Sinclair's conclusion is that language is not the source of logic, but, rather, is structured by logic. She says, "In our view . . . the way in which sensorimotor schemes, coordinated into practical groups, become transformed into operations would determine the manner in which linguistic structures are acquired" (1969, p. 333). This would imply that a sensorimotor underpinning is necessary for linguistic structures, and with this statement we would agree. Meanings for *up, down; more, less;* coordinates, conditionals, etc., are all acquired through the sensorimotor system. This conclusion, however, begs the question of whether language training, and particularly syntactical training, can *aid* the development of logical operations, when combined with the activity of the child. (Note that Sinclair found it harder to teach syntactical structures, like comparatives and coordinates, than lexical or vocabulary items).

And we can find strong signals in the research evidence available that language mediation can be effective. In fact, we can identify in certain studies specific syntactical structures used in training. Beilin (1965), and Smith's (1968) follow-up of Beilin, showed that verbal rule instruction phrased as an inference is an effective training procedure. In the training, an incorrect conservation of weight response was followed by an *if—then* statement, "*If* we start with a ball of plasticene and we don't put any pieces of plasticene on it, or take any pieces away from it, *then* it still weighs the same even though it looks different. See, I can make it back into a ball so it hasn't really changed." The repeated statement of a guiding principle using the syntax of inference for a total of 12 trials accelerated formation of conservation. However, it may be, as Beilin suggests, that *verbal rule instruction* provides only a *model* for a solution; the technique did not prove to be resistant to counter suggestion. In a later study by Beilin (1965) on a water level representation task (a task where the child is asked to show on the outline of a bottle what the water level of a half-filled bottle of water would look like if the bottle were tilted on its side), verbal training was effective, although training in anticipation imagery was more so, perhaps because of the special nature of this task.

Kohnstamm (1967) used verbal instruction to train children on a class inclusion task. His technique was to explain the problem to the child who gave the wrong answer, using the syntax of causality, so that children would learn the thought operation. For example, if a child said, in response to a question, that there were more policemen than men, the experimenter would say, "No, that's not right. You're supposed to say that there are more men because policemen are also men." The lessons were most effective when verbal training in causal expressions was combined with the use of blocks and pictures. It would be well to underscore, at this point, the fact that Kohnstamm *combined* verbal training with a training procedure involving self-activity on the child's part. Piaget's recent work on causality, to which reference has been made, shows how loosely the child uses the word *because*. Teaching the child to use the word is not going to make the child more logical, but providing opportunity for the child to experience cause-and-effect relationships through self-activity and *then* supplying the syntactical forms (including use of the past, present and future tenses to express a temporal sequence) may support the logical structures as they begin to emerge.

A more direct approach to acceleration through syntactical training has been used successfully by Sigel and colleagues (1966). His training procedure is derived from the Piagetian thesis that complex operations are built upon simpler ones and that conservation is possible only when the mental operations of multiple classification, multiple seriation, and reversibility are present. The syntactical structures involved here were complex noun-phrases (*small, brown leaf*); comparatives (*larger than; darker than*); disjoints (leaves can be small and not brown) and conjunctives (leaves can be small *and* brown). Training involved having children learn two or more attributes of an object, combining these to define another class, and reorganizing categories to return to the original. The training program over a five-week period proved to be effective.

Greenfield (1969) tried various procedures for helping children acquire the concept of roundness and squareness through linguistic training. Some procedures involved using the word *square,* for example, in a variety of contexts; some in a single verbal context. Each of these was combined with a procedure for correcting errors by using a contractive term to *square* or by not introducing contractive terms. Pre— and post—test scores for experimental and control groups showed that the largest improvement was registered by the group exposed both to the term *square* in a variety of verbal and action contexts and to contractive terms when they made errors. Greenfield is critical of preschool approaches that have emphasized direct experience with materials and have left unspecified the communicative context in which all such experience must take place. She concludes that what is said about concrete experience is more important in the semantic development of analytic terms than the nature of the experience itself.

Additional light on the relationship between language and logic is found in research reported by Clark (1969). He hypothesized that the solution of certain problems involving deductive reasoning is accomplished mainly through very general linguistic processes. The reasoning problems he referred to are of the type, "If John is better than Dick, and Pete is worse than Dick, then who is best?" Four stages were identified by Clark in the solution of such problems: comprehension of the propositions, comprehension of the question, search for information asked for on the question, and construction of the answer.

From psycholinguistic theory, Clark derived some interesting principles that can be used to determine how difficult a statement will be to comprehend. The principles specify what it is the listener knows of a sentence he has heard, and how he searches his memory for the wanted knowledge. One principle is that functional relations, like those of subject, verb, and direct object, are stored in the memory in a more readily available form than other kinds of information, like that of theme.

When subject, verb and direct object are integrated within a sentence so that few, if any, transformations are necessary, the sentence takes less time to understand and less space in immediate memory. The sentence, "John saw Pete" is therefore easier to understand than "Pete is seen by John." And, "Children who have finished their work may get ready for juice" is more complex than "Finish your work and get ready for juice."

The second principle is that the sense of certain words like *good* and *long* is stored in the memory in a less complex form than the sense of their opposites. Someone who asks, "How *good* is the food?" is merely asking for an evaluation of the food. But when someone asks, "How *bad* is the food?" he has already made a judg-

ment that the food is bad and is asking about the extent of its badness. The proposition that "John is *better than* Pete" is easier to
understand than the proposition, "Pete is *worse than* Dick." In the
latter proposition, the listener realizes that both Pete and Dick are
bad more readily than he realizes that Pete is more extreme than
Dick in his badness.

The third principle is that information cannot be retrieved from
a sentence unless it is congruent in its functional relations with the
information being sought. The answer to the question, "*If* John is
better than Pete, then *who* is *best?*" ("bad English" according to
some standards, but useful in Clark's research), is immediately
forthcoming—"John is *best.*" But if the question is asked in a different form from the statement, as in, "*Who is worst?*" then the prob-
lem-solver must transform the question to *who is least good* and
search his memory for the information.

Clark tested students on various forms of the *A is better than B;
B is better than C* type problem and found, in general, that his
hypotheses with respect to which wording would be easiest were
confirmed. His researches, as well as those of other investigators
working on similar problems, gave us insight into the difficulties
children can have in grasping the information in certain types of
statements. They also lend support to the position that, since the
linguistic process is inextricably bound up with the reasoning process, a training program to combine both processes would be more
effective than training for one alone. We shall now examine programs designed to combine training on both linguistic and reasoning processes.

PROGRAMS TO IMPROVE LANGUAGE DEVELOPMENT

One of the widely publicized approaches to improve language
development is that in which English is taught as if children were
learning a second language. In parts of large metropolitan areas
populated by Puerto Ricans and in the Southwest with large popu-
lations of Spanish-American or Indian children, English may indeed be a second language. Even where it is not, however, some
investigators maintain that the children's handicap is sufficiently

great to warrant a drastic new approach to language teaching, an approach which is patterned after contemporary methods of teaching foreign languages.

Basic to the teaching method is the patterned drill. Two educational psychologists, Bereiter and Engelmann (1966) developed a preschool program for disadvantaged four-year-old children which relies solely upon patterned drill. The program has been so widely publicized that it will not be described in detail here. To review briefly, fifteen subjects received three twenty-minute periods of instruction a day in subject-matter areas—language, arithmetic and reading. All three subjects were taught by the same method, that of having children repeat statement patterns; all instruction was verbal and no toys or other concrete objects were used. For example, language instruction began by teaching children basic identity patterns by verbatim repetition:

1. *Verbatim repetition:*
   Teacher: This block is red. Say it . . . .
   Children: This block is red.
2. *Yes-no questions:*
   Teacher: Is this block red?
   Children: No, this block is not red.
3. *Location tasks:*
   Teacher: Show me a block that is red.
   Children: This block is red.
4. *Statement production:*
   Teacher: Tell me about this piece of chalk.
   Children: This piece of chalk is red.
   Teacher: Tell me about what this piece of chalk is *not.*
   Children: (ad lib) This piece of chalk is not green . . . not blue, etc.
5. *Deduction problems:*
   Teacher: (With piece of chalk hidden in hand) This piece of chalk is not red. Do you know what color it is?
   Children: No, Maybe it is blue . . . maybe it is yellow . . . .
   (p. 134)

Bereiter reports that it takes four-year-old children considerable time to learn these statement patterns with their plural variations and sub-class nouns, (e.g., "This animal is a tiger"). The length of time varies considerably—from six or seven months for those with practically no spoken language to two or three months for those of near normal language competence, at the end of which time the children can recite such statements as "If it's a hammer, then it's a tool" which purportedly illustrates proficiency in class inclusion (knowing that "hammer" is a subclass in the more general class, "tool") and in inferring (knowing that *if* something is true, *then* we can infer that something else is true).

Critics of such an approach to language training argue that the grammatical sentences children give are evidence of response learning; they doubt that patterned drill affects language and thought processes any more effectively than memorizing nursery rhymes and learning to respond, "Dickory comes after Hickory," and, "The mouse ran down the clock; the mouse did not run up the clock."

Critics of patterned drill also contend that it is too limited a program. In language lessons, for example, the children in patterned drill classes are exposed to a very limited variety of syntactical forms including a limited number of verbs, mostly in the present tense. Yet we know that human beings have a natural capacity for language and acquire it often in the face of great difficulties. With sufficient exposure to a rich vocabulary and a complex syntax in interactions with adults, children can process data and put together utterances which they have never heard themselves. If a mother says to her three-year-old, "Find Daddy and tell him supper is ready," the child does not find his father and say, "Find Daddy and tell him supper is ready," as a child might parrot in a patterned drill. Instead, he says to his father, "Daddy, Mommy says supper is ready." Young children acquire the structure of the language by listening to what is said to them, processing the information, figuring out the rules, and *using what they have figured out in reply*.

Some support for the "natural" method of language training is to be found in Cazden's research. Cazden (1965) exposed a small group of preschool children to a treatment she called "modeling"; that is, a tutor would reply to a child's utterances in a conversational manner, modeling as she did so a rich variety of syntactical forms. While differences between modeling and a second treatment were not significant, results favored modeling.

But the natural method of acquiring language is effective only if the child has sufficient chance to interact with adults who use language effectively. Jensen (1968), who has been a major investigator in the area of language learning, states, "The degree of subtlety, diversity, and complexity of the verbal environment will determine the nature of the syntactical processes incorporated by the developing child. The extent to which these structures become incorporated is a function of the frequency with which they are experienced in the environment, the degree to which the social environment reinforces their overt manifestation, and the individual's basic capacity for learning."

In Cazden's research, the tutor worked with *three* children at a time, and there was no attempt to structure the language training. Comparing her research with Blank's raises interesting questions.

Blank (1968) provided training on a one-to-one basis and makes a strong case for such a tutorial language program. She points out that the usual classroom situation does not require overt responses by the child; the teacher gives directions to which the child does not have to perform verbally and which he can carry out by imitating other students. In a one-to-one tutorial session with the teacher, the teacher can not only ensure that the child uses language, but she can also plan the tutorial sessions to meet the special needs of the child. Blank sees these needs as related to the child's deficit in abstract thinking and has developed a program in which abilities are developed such as attending selectively to phenomena, dealing with exclusions, categorizing, dealing with cause and effect, separating words from their referents, etc. Blank reported gains of 14 IQ points for children tutored for 15 to 20 minutes daily over a four month period.

The question of number of children to receive training at a time and the question of kind of training are interrelated. When children are moving freely about the room, it is difficult for the teacher to carry on a conversation with more than one at a time. The situation is easier when children are seated around a table, engaged in a common enterprise that is language-provoking. It is possible under such circumstances for the teacher to carry on interactions with groups of four, five or six children (depending upon age and need) during the same session.

Granted that language training should take place in small groups so that there is considerable adult-child interaction; granted that in the training the child should be exposed to a rich variety of syntactical forms and, particularly, those that might conceivably aid logical development; how can such training be systematized so as to make sure that what is known about language and logical development is fully utilized? Many present preschool programs leave everything up to the teacher, who may not be aware of the tremendous amount of knowledge about language development accumulated in the last few years. Too many present research programs decide the content of the training program on the basis of whatever items the investigator thinks to be important. Thus, thousands of children in the country are being trained on a few limited syntactical forms and a few limited logical operations the choice of which is personal to the investigator and, indeed, whimsical.

A systematic approach should have a firm foundation in theory. It should be based upon a grand plan of how intellectual development takes place, a plan that is adequately supported by research. Fortunately, in the area of logical development, such a grand plan is available in the developmental theory of Piaget. We can take what he has discovered about the emergence of schemes of classification, space and number, and seriation and build a training program upon it. And in the area of syntactical structures, we can turn to the field of developmental psycholinguistics for an analysis of syntax and how syntactical forms emerge.

Bellugi-Klima (1967), for example, has studied the emergence of negation in the speech of the young child. First it appears that the child negates by commencing sentences with "No" as in, "No can do it"; "No get jelly"; next the child positions *no, not, don't* or *can't* in a sentence, but not always grammatically, as in, "He not waking up." A new development is the appearance of multiple negation, with the child sprinkling several negatives in one sentence: "No one didn't took it." Tag questions appear still later. In the sentence, "You understand, don't you?," "don't you" is a tag. Tag questions are quite involved, for the child must make a decision about affirmative and negative forms. If the sentence is negative, the tag is affirmative: "He isn't here, is he?" If the sentence is affirmative, the tag is negative: "He's here, isn't he?" The child must make a decision about number and gender, using singular or plural, masculine, feminine or neuter, as the sentence demands.

The field of study concerned with the development of language forms as they emerge during the early years is called *developmental psycholinguistics*. From this relatively new but fascinating field we can identify the syntactical forms with which children are likely to need help. Some of those that have been identified to date and their relevance for education include: (Bellugi-Klima and Hass, 1968)

1. *Inflections denoting plurals, past tense endings, and third person singular present indicative.* Example: The beads are round. We pour*ed* the water. The number of pennies match*es* the number of bottles.

Disadvantaged children in particular need help here. Studies of speech patterns of Puerto Rican children in New York City call attention to the absence of these inflections in junior high students; their omission can create difficulties in reading comprehension. The child who does not use *ed* to mark the past tense may slough over the *ed* in print and fail to distinguish between actions occurring in the past and present.

2. *Prepositions such as "behind", "in", "on", "over", etc.* The precise meaning of these "little" words which nevertheless encode considerable information is often lost on the young child.

3. *Auxiliary verbs.* Studies show that *helping verbs* like the *has* in "has gone" are often missing in the speech of disadvantaged children, yet like inflections, such verb forms add more information to a sentence. "He gone" might mean "He has gone," "He will have gone," or any number of other meanings.

4. *Coordinators such as "and" that connect two grammatical elements in a conjoining transformation.* Here the difficulty may be in short-term memory. If the teacher says, "Put the red beads here," even the very young child can do it. If the teacher next says, "Put the blue beads here, also," the child can also follow the directions. But when the teacher connects the two ideas, "Put the red beads here and the blue beads here," the very young child may place only the blue. Older preschool children may not be able to follow more complicated statements involving coordination

such as, "Finish cleaning up your table and then go along to the bathroom."

5. *Adversatives where one idea is the opposite or the antithesis of another. But* is an adversative conjunction, as in the sentence, "It's small *but* heavy." We expect small objects to be light, and when an opposing idea is added instead, the "heavy" may be lost.

6. *Disjoint where a class may be taken apart and the elements making up the class separated from one another.* An example of a disjoint is the statement, "Show me the beads that are red and not square."

7. *Comparatives. More, less; lighter, darker; shorter, taller,* are examples of comparative forms which are essential for putting objects in some kind of order.

8. *Complex Nounphrases.* The use of *modifiers* such as "the short, narrow piece"; "jagged, rough, uneven objects" aids in precise description and definition of properties of objects.

9. *Relative Clauses.* The directions of teachers often include such modifying clauses as "Whatever beads you can't sort, you can put to one side." The construction is a useful one in describing an object precisely.

10. *Temporal Connectives.* Connectives such as *when, after, until, as soon as* which indicate time appear late in language development. Teachers of young children know that a statement such as, "When you have finished, you can get ready for juice," is usually the signal for children to move in on the juice.

11. *Conditional Statements. If—then* type statements as expressed in, "If you put the longer one here, then where should the shorter one go?"

It is possible to model each of these forms systematically in the course of the structured lessons. Consider a small group of children in a tutorial session working on classification, space and number, or seriation activities. The teacher in the course of that session can model one or more forms selected for that session. For example, as children arrange rods in order of size the teacher would make sure that she used comparatives as often as possible in such questions as, "Which is longer, this one or this one?" "Which is fatter, this one or this one?" To elicit comparatives from the children, she might say, "Tell me about these two rods. What can you say about how long this one is compared to the other? What can you say about this other one?" If the child makes no response or says, "It's blue," the teacher can supply the form she's trying to elicit saying, "Yes it's blue; it's also taller than this one. Now tell me about this one (holding up the smaller)." She does not insist upon a verbatim copy of what she has said, but only that the child use the comparative form correctly in his reply. Or the teacher might model a complex noun-phrase such as, "Find a picture of a large, furry animal"; "Show me a small, white, baby shoe," and then elicit, by a question, a statement from a child where he had to use such a grammatical construction.

The modeling and eliciting procedure grows out of the assumption that children of the poor have not heard enough such syntactical structures directed to them to which they must react. The procedure demands that children listen to the statement, process the input and construct a verbal response. Constructing a verbal response is much more difficult than decoding meaning from a spoken statement. If one is studying French, it is much easier to figure out the meaning of the statement, "On peut étudier la perception de nombreux points de vue, dont le plus classique est le point de vue psycho-physiologique," than to state in English, "one can study perception from a number of points of view, of which the most classic is the psycho-physiological."

Will modeling and eliciting syntactical structures in the course of small group lessons guarantee their usage in spontaneous speech? The answer seems to be, "No." In studies by Hart and Risley (in press), small group teaching affected color-noun and number-noun combinations in the group teaching situation but was ineffective in changing the rates of usage in the children's spontaneous vocabularies. The teacher must also use modeling and eliciting as children engage in spontaneous, self-directed activities during free play periods. She can make access to materials contingent upon the use of complex noun phrases or ask questions of children to elicit other structures. However, the procedure will defeat its purpose if it is conducted in a drill-type manner. Rather, it should be conducted so that an observer in the classroom would hear only a natural conversation between teacher and pupil. When children have to verbalize, mental activity is encouraged. The child can be neither a passive audience with words "going in one ear and out the other" nor a parrot mimicking exactly what he has heard. The procedure demands that the learner be mentally active which, as Piaget points out, is essential to cognitive growth.

Caution must be exerted that eliciting occurs in a warm, friendly, supportive manner. Sharp insistence on a child's repeating exactly what the teacher said or correcting his every response will make verbal communication distasteful to him and turn him off. Dr. O. Hobart Mowrer, worked with birds to discover the conditions under which parrots, mynah birds and other talking birds learned to talk. He found that a bird learned best when the caretaker acted as a good "mother" to the bird, talking to the bird as he fed it, so the bird learned to associate talking with the good things of life. A child who hears language continually directed to him in a critical, rejecting way is not going to be motivated to change speech patterns.

Assuming that a modeling-eliciting procedure will be successful in establishing certain grammatical structures in the child's language, we next ask, "What possible contribution can these structures make to cognitive growth?" As we have pointed out, Piaget argues, and we believe rightly so, that logical thinking precedes logical expression of ideas. However, the teaching-learning procedures that we have described are conducive to accurate verbalization by the child: he learns the structures to use in describing properties dealing with quantities, making comparisons, etc., and there is some evidence that such verbalization aids learning. Jensen and his students (1965) have conducted a number of experiments which reveal that syntactical verbal behavior is of great psychological importance to learning and intellectual ability. They found that retarded junior high school students could learn a list of paired-associates (shoe-clock, telephone-hammer) more successfully when the list was presented in sentences, "I threw the shoe at the clock;" "I smashed the telephone with the hammer," than by naming items alone. Also, attaching verbal labels such as *more* or *less* to cognitive structures may help to reinforce the structure and develop a learning set that can be used in many different situations.

While there is still much to be learned about language development and language training, we know enough from the present state of the art to put together at least tentatively what should go into a model for language training. The model should incorporate these features:

1. Some language training should be provided in small group sessions, so as to maximize opportunity for two-way conversations between teacher and child.

2. In the small group sessions, the teacher should serve as a model, presenting to children in her own speech a variety of well-formed sentences.

3. Not only should the teacher model certain syntactical structures for children; she should also elicit from them those structures she is modeling, or an approximation of them.

4. Modeling and eliciting should be carried on in a natural, conversational manner during periods of free play, as well as in small group sessions.

5. In choosing syntactical structures to model, the teacher should keep in mind two factors: the level of difficulty of the structure in relationship to the child's own linguistic development, and the possible contribution of the structure to logical thinking.

6. Language training should be carried on in a warm, friendly, supportive environment with the teacher relying more on modeling than on correcting so that the child's associations with language are pleasant ones, and he will more likely be motivated to use language well.

Herb Weitman, University City Public Schools, University City, Missouri

Child engages in a classification activity designed to foster multiple classification. To match the model string of beads prepared by the teacher, the
child must keep in mind several variables: color, shape, number and size.

4. Development of Classification Operations

CURRENT PRESCHOOL programs that emphasize cognitive development include in their curriculum activities hopefully designed to teach classification. Yet, teachers are not always clear as to why such activities are important and what relationship exists between classification skills and reasoning processes. Those who raise the question may be thinking of classification skills in terms of memorizing formal biological schemes in high school or college which haven't proved particularly useful, or of carrying out assignments involving the listing of items by categories. If this were all there was to classification, teachers' questions would be justified. However, the ability to classify is important because it is essential to dealing economically with the environment. We put a pencil in a glass of water and observe how it appears to bend. Is this particular phenomenon an example of magic or of how light behaves when it travels from one medium to another? If we assign the phenomenon to the latter class, then we know that the same laws apply here as apply to other examples of light traveling through two media. A five-year-old is sitting on the edge of a car seat without his seat belt fastened. The car stops suddenly and the child shoots *forward* and hits the back of the front seat. Is this an isolated instance, or can we assign it to the class of all objects in motion continuing in the direction of motion? Can we classify it as an example of Newton's First Law, which will be repeated again and again given similar conditions? Being able to acquire concepts or generalizations makes it easier and more economical to deal with new phenomena, and classification is inextricably bound up with acquiring concepts.

As Elkind (1969) points out, classification responses help to maintain the psychic economy by eliminating the need for fresh adaptations every time a new object is encountered. New phenomena can be assigned to a particular class and dealt with efficiently, instead of having to be mastered individually. Montessori, in fact, placed so much importance upon classification that she identified intelligence with the faculty of classification; "to be able to distinguish, classify and catalogue on the basis of a secure order established in the mind, this is at once intelligence and culture" (Kohlberg, 1968).

Programs for young children typically include classification activities of two types. One type involves sorting, usually on a perceptual level. For example, the teacher may ask the child to find all the red objects in a collection of different colored objects, or all the large objects, or all the round objects, or all objects possessing some other property readily perceived through the senses. Such training exercises may stem from Montessori's belief that the faculty for classifying developed as a result of sensory training—of providing opportunity to discriminate differences in color, shape, size, pitch and texture. From such sensory experiences abstract concepts like "squareness" would emerge, thus providing a basis for classification. Unfortunately, however, at least to a Piagetian, if the child has made the association of red with particular sensory stimuli, he can immediately zero in on the proper objects and solve the problem with no mental operations involved.

A variation of classifying by sensory stimuli is one where children are asked to find similarities or differences. They may be shown a series of objects and asked to find an object which differs from the others—a cat with one ear in a row of cats with two ears, or a flower with an odd-shaped petal amidst flowers with normal petals. Activities of this kind have formed the backbone of reading readiness programs, presumably because they train the child to recognize likenesses and differences in words. The claim is made that such activities also provide training for classification, since classification also involves recognition of likenesses and differences. Actually, these activities have limited value for both purposes.

According to Piagetian theory, there is serious doubt that such exercises in sensory training stimulate intellectual growth. To discriminate "redness" or "roughness" demands merely a perceptual judgment; one takes in information via the eye or the hand and categorizes the information. Involved are no mental operations like reversing thought processes or combining bits of information to solve a problem. For Piaget, perceptual structures and cognitive structures are two quite different structures of the mind; he finds perceptual structures to be rigid and relatively unchanged by experience. (See pp. 41-42) We see red as red, once we learn the label for our sensory experience, unless we are color-blind, and our perception of the color does not change from early childhood on. Piaget's students have found that perceptual rigidity characterizes certain classical illusions, like >——< <——>. Adults are no better than children in assessing equality of length in such stimuli, except that adults may have learned to be cautious.

True classification demands more than perceptual judgments; it demands mental operations. The child must not only take in information, but he must also remake the information. Most children up to the age of about six make judgments on the basis of how things look to them; with the onset of operational structures they become capable of reversing thought processes, of making logical comparisons, of knowing the conditions under which things are the same and different.

Sometimes sorting activities involve activity on a conceptual level, with concepts typically defined in terms of function. Directions to the child may be: "Find all the objects we can sit on; find all the things that we can eat; find all the things that we can wear; find all the things to ride in." These definitions of concepts or classes of things are typical of the kind of definitions by *use* that children give on the Binet test of intelligence, and provoked an amusing book of such definitions, several years ago, entitled, *A Hole is to Dig*. As Elkind (1969) points out, such definitions are correct in a certain sense, but are hardly the criteria on which a child bases his classification. Assignments based upon such definitions are extremely limited in terms of aiding logical development.

They ignore the essence of classification, which is *abstracting* the *common property* in a group of objects or experiences and *extending* the *class* to include *all* objects and experiences possessing that common property.

CLASSIFICATION BEHAVIOR

Inhelder and Piaget have traced the development of logical classification from its origins in infancy. Even during the first year of life we can find evidence that the infant is building schemes or structures under which he can classify new phenomena. One such schema appears to be built around suspended objects; the infant apparently recognizes that such objects swing when pushed, and he sets a new toy over his crib in motion by a push. Or, he opens his mouth wide at the same time that he pries open a match box, indicating thereby the existence of a generalized notion of "opening" to which he assigns the new phenomenon—the match box. Schemata or structures built out of past experiences make it possible for the infant to deal with a new object or experience by putting it under existing schema. Classification here is at a sensorimotor level; the infant "knows" with his sensorimotor system.

By two years of age, children are capable of making what Piaget calls "graphic collections." Given a set of elements, like cut-outs of circles, squares and triangles, with the instructions to "put together the things which are alike" or "things that go together in some way," the child tends to make a spatial arrangement out of the objects. He may line up the circles and a triangle and call the line a train and then arrange squares and triangles in a group and call them a house. There is no preliminary plan; the child establishes a similarity between the first element chosen and the second, but then he appears to be carried away by what the arrangement reminds him of and proceeds with a construction that ignores the task he has been asked to do. This kind of behavior persists for a year or more; even three- and four-year-olds do not appear able to foresee the result they are aiming at while the action is in progress. Their behavior can best be explained by "chaining," where one response serves as the stimulus for the next, rather than each response fitting into a preconceived plan.

True or logical classification involves both intension and extension: hindsight and anticipation. We know the intension of a class when we know the properties common to that class; we can deal with its extension when we can include in the class all objects or experiences possessing the common properties defined by its intension. We must have hindsight in keeping in mind the common properties, and we must have foresight or anticipation in extending the class to the series of objects and situations to which it can be applied. Memory is obviously important (and it is interesting in this connection to note the extensive work done in recent years in Geneva [Inhelder, 1969] on memory), but hindsight is more than a matter of remembering a set of properties. What goes on in the mind is a sort of reappraisal in which objects are continually being sorted as they are scanned.

We give the child some geometrical shapes, circles and squares, red and blue, large and small, and ask him to sort them into two piles, those alike in one particular way in one pile, and those alike but in a different way in another pile; he is directed to think up piles so that he uses every single shape. The child scans the shapes and decides upon color (red or blue) as the criterion. This is the intension of the class to be kept in mind as he looks for every element, regardless of its shape and size, possessing the color criterion, either red or blue, that he began with. Can he include all of the elements in one of these two piles? If not, then he must discard color as a common property since his assignment requires him to classify all elements into one of the two groups. If you, the reader, will do the activity in your own mind, you will appreciate the mental operations that are involved in classificatory behavior. The mind is very active, setting up a tentative hypothesis with respect to the common property, testing each object against that criterion, disregarding any distracting irrelevant properties like shape and size, and ascertaining that all elements possessing the common property have been chosen.

Note the difference between this kind of activity and that described previously where the child was asked to find all objects of the same color, or all of the red objects. In this latter type of assignment, the *teacher* has done the classifying; *she* has carried on the mental operations of abstracting the common property and deciding on the intension of the class. If the child knows the names of colors, he can carry out the assignment on a purely sensory level, with no mental activity involved.

Unless the teacher is aware of the existence and importance of mental operations in true classification, it is all too easy to waste children's time in carrying out assignments that are merely busy work. The teacher has a job of classifying to do here, in arriving at decisions as to whether or not a task can be solved perceptually.

It is easy to overlook a cue. One teacher found that her class of disadvantaged five-year-olds was breezing through a problem that she had thought would provide challenging practice in class inclusion. Each of the children had been given a set of miniature toys— a cow, a horse, a duck, a fish, a robin, a house, a barn, a garage, etc., and was asked to make two different groups out of the toys, each group alike in some way. The teacher had in mind a classification of "animal" and "shelter;" she had thought the task would be hard because children would not include ducks, fish and robins with mammals such as the cow and horse to form the class of animals, nor "garage" and "barn" as shelters of a sort. Instead, the children completed the task successfully in a very short time. All of the animals were made of white plastic; this property was so striking that it was easy for the children to select objects made of white plastic for one group and to put all other objects in a second group. There are excellent classification activities that can be carried on with objects differing in color, but one color must not be such a strong visual stimulus that it is easily differentiated.

The characteristics of logical classification have been described by Inhelder and Piaget (1964, p. 48). Those of particular concern to teachers of young children are:

1. There are no isolated elements, i.e., elements not belonging to a class. If an element is the only one of its kind, then it gives rise to its own specific class.

2. For every specific class, there is a complementary class characterized by the property of not having the property of the specific class. The class of fruit, for example, might be said to consist of oranges and all the fruit-not-oranges. For the class of wire-haired dogs, we have the class of dogs-not-wire-haired.

3. A specific class includes *all* the members having the property common to that class.

4. A specific class includes *only* members having the property common to that class.

5. The class of things that belong both to *A*'s and not *A*'s is the empty set. Or, there is no such thing as a dog belonging to neither the class of wire-haired or the class of dogs-not-wire-haired.

6. A complementary class has its own characteristics.

7. A particular class is included in every higher ranking class which contains all its elements: "all" *A* or "some" *B*.

With these characteristics of classification in mind, it is possible to construct a model of a training program to foster development of logical classification. First, the characteristics listed above have to be translated into separate operations, and then the operations must be arranged in order of difficulty to match as nearly as possible a developmental sequence.

For children to be able to carry on classification activities according to the logic of the characteristics mentioned they must be capable of certain mental operations. They have to be able to take in information from an object or experience in the environment and transform that information, *do* something to it, as follows:

1. Identifying properties of objects (size, color, shape, etc.), and matching objects by more than one property.

2. Keeping in mind two or more properties of objects at the same time while searching for any object to complete a set.

3. Combining objects to make up subclasses and combining subclasses to make supra-classes, and recognizing the existence of complementary classes.

4. Changing from one criterion for grouping to another.

5. Taking a whole class apart to find subclasses, and making comparisons of "all" and "some".

6. Discovering intension and extension of a class.

7. Visualizing an object as having simultaneous membership in two classes.

8. Putting together elements from several groups so that none is repeated.

9. Making all possible combinations of elements.

What kind of training experiences might conceivably foster the development of these operations? We shall describe a set, together with the rationale for the choice, and what to anticipate in the way of child reaction to the experiences.

THE TRAINING PROGRAM

1. *Identifying properties of objects and matching objects by more than one property*

Children vary considerably in their ability to use correct labels for such properties as size, color and shape. A child's senses will *tell* him that he is not looking at the same thing when he sees first a red circle and then a yellow one; or first a red circle and then a red square; or first a large red square and then a small red square. However, he must learn the names for what he is seeing. He accomplishes the task through associative learning, that is, by hearing the name often enough when he is observing one of the properties. And, as Greenfield (1969) has pointed out, presenting the key word in a variety of verbal and action contexts, and using contractive terms when children make errors appears to be effective in teaching properties..

In *Early Childhood Curriculum — A Piaget Approach,* we go beyond the mere naming of properties. The goals for the set of activities include not only identifying properties of objects, but also matching objects by more than one property. The equipment used is a specially selected set of kindergarten beads, in two sizes, two shapes and three colors. The teacher makes a model string and the children copy the string. Activities are sequenced, beginning with the very simple one where the child is instructed to make a necklace by stringing *all* the *red* beads on a shoelace. He does the other colors in turn and, in subsequent lessons, shapes and sizes. Next, he must copy models that the teacher makes, models that begin with a simple alternation of red bead with yellow bead and end with a complex pattern demanding that the child attend to number, size, shape and color of beads all at the same time.

The over-all objective of having children identify properties of objects and match objects by more than one property is to have children be able to find the common property of a class and to extend that class to include all objects possessing that property. Thus, the teacher may vary directions on subsequent days to say,

"Find all the beads that are alike in some way and string them," and, "Tell me how they're alike."

Accompanying the actions are verbal activities, with the teacher presenting models of certain grammatical structures. As with the actions the child carries out, grammatical structures modeled for him are sequenced, beginning with simple declarative sentences and progressing to transformations upon those sentences to include coordinate sentences with directions for more than one action. In each case, after the teacher gives the directions and the child begins the action, the teacher says, "Tell me what you're doing. Why did you choose that one?" This exercise forces the child to attend to not one, but several properties of an object at the same time, and to describe the object using noun phrases: "It's a round bead;" or, "it's a small yellow bead." If the child cannot put words together to frame a response properly, the teacher models the correct response and asks him to repeat it. This he may not do letter-perfect; research on imitation shows that children will repeat correctly only those grammatical structures which they already have in their repertoire (Slobin, 1969).

There are follow-up activities to be carried out in connection with each set of materials designed to reinforce and extend what has been taught. For example, in one, two children may be hidden from each other's view by a screen. One child puts a bead on his screen, and says to the other, "I'm putting on a round yellow bead" (note use of noun phrase, with adjectives to describe two properties). The other child then puts a round yellow bead on his string, plus another which he describes to his unseen companion, and the game continues for a specified number of beads, at the end of which time children can physically compare their strings. A number of investigators have commented on the need to have children use the language of referents—to talk about events and objects not visible or not in the immediate present. The follow-up activity just described provides training for this very important skill.

2. *Keeping in mind two or more properties of objects in searching for an object to complete a set*

This activity in the Piagetian program requires that the child put to use the skill developed in the beads activity; he must keep two or more properties of objects in mind as he searches for an object to complete a set. The vehicle of instruction is the matrix puzzle. A matrix is an ordered series of elements designed in such a manner that the elements in one pair are related to the elements in another in the same way. Readers are familiar with matrices in intelligence test items: "Black is to white as night is to . . . . ," and the subject must supply the necessary word. The puzzles in this program are picture puzzles; the first in the series makes use of the training in recognizing properties of size, shape and color provided in the beads activity. The picture shows one large red flower and one small yellow flower in the top horizontal row, and one large red apple and a blank space for which the child must select a card picturing one small yellow apple from a number of choices of flowers and apples. The puzzles become increasingly difficult, demanding attention to three variables at the same time. At first glance, an adult is likely to think that the puzzle is too difficult for the preschool child, that he will not be able to follow the verbal directions. This, however, is not the case. The young child can solve the puzzle without too much difficulty; the trouble is that he solves it at a perceptual level rather than a conceptual one. Inhelder and Piaget (1964) describe how the child uses symmetry to do this. Instead of thinking of how each of the first pictured pair of objects is related and finding a picture that will establish the same relationship in another pair, he simply thinks "I've got a red one here, and this one's yellow, so the answer card must be yellow. And there's one here and one here and one here, so it's got to be one here." By a simple matching of elements that stand out perceptually, he can solve the puzzle.

How can one find out at what level the child is operating? Ask him. This is what Inhelder and Piaget did and what the Piagetian program described here urges teachers to do. Furthermore, when the teacher says, "Tell me about it. Why did you choose that card?" she is developing both language and logic. With many children, such a question is often greeted with a look of surprise, as if this were the first time the child had been asked to explain his action to another person. Regardless of the answer, the teacher then selects another answer card, puts it in place of the child's choice and asks, "Would this one do just as well?" "In what way?"

or "Why?" We have found in our experimental work that time and time again a child who has chosen the correct card without hesitation will abandon his choice also without hesitation and justify the incorrect response by finding a different symmetry. If he cannot think in terms of two variables at once, he will agree to any choice card containing one of the properties in question.

Again, language can help to emphasize that an object can have several properties at the same time. The teacher says, "Tell me about this picture. What does it show?" If the child responds with "Two red flowers," the teacher asks, "Are they large or small?" and may model the correct sentence, "There are two large red flowers." She models "small yellow flower," also, and then reviews: "There are two large red flowers and a small yellow flower in the top row. If we want the next row to go with the top row in the same way, and we start with apples, then we have two large red apples and a .... What two things do we have to remember about the apple to make it go with the flower?" Pointing to the objects as she emphasizes the relationship that must be maintained provides the visual image for the words she is using.

3. *Complementary classes*

The next set of activities in the series is designed to provide training in the ability to recognize complementary classes. Given pictures of dogs of which two are collies (or "Lassies" as the children call them) can the children separate the set into collies and dogs-not-collies? The object is to make *two* classes of dogs, no more. The young child may make collections of as many classes as there are kinds of dogs, but this is not the task. In fact, teachers who are new to teaching classification skills often characterize such behavior as "creative"; they remark proudly on the number of classes the child can think of. Actually, such behavior is more characteristic of the younger child; it is not at all difficult to match dog for dog on a perceptual basis. A much more creative task is demanded of the child in dealing with complementary classes.

The actual materials used in our Piagetian program were an assortment of miniature vehicles consisting of trucks, airplanes and a car, to make up the class of *trucks* and the complementary class of *things not-trucks*. Since the vehicles were in three colors, it was possible also to form a class of *red* objects and a complementary class of *objects-not-red* or, more simply, *other objects*. As Inhelder and Piaget explain (1964), the relationship here is important in helping children understand what is included in a class: that when we talk about collies or airplanes, there is understood a complementary class of dogs-not-collies or vehicles-not-planes, and that both the specified class and its complement make up the total class. The reader may have noted how often adults will completely disregard the complementary class in discussing a specified class and, as a result, make illogical remarks.

Inhelder and Piaget point out that the relation of a class to its complement is also important because it raises the more general problem of negation. In order to perform the dichotomy required of him in this set of activities, the child is forced to divide a variety of objects into a class *and* its complement, with the complement being described negatively. The authors describe what happens at different age levels. Two- and three-year-olds construct a dichotomy which observes no rules of classification. Given pictures of various fruits, they might put an apple, a grape, a lemon or a melon in one collection, and cherries, apples, a pear and a banana in the other. From five years of age on, children divide objects into two collections, but some try to define the second collection positively rather than negatively. For example, the child will put together a class of apples using all the pictures of apples in front of him, and then put all the pictures of other fruits in another class but define that second class as "pears" or "bananas" or "apples and fruit," as if one term did not include the other. Children who solve the problem correctly call the second class, "other kinds of fruit," or "fruits that aren't apples," showing that they are able to take classes apart and recombine them for a given purpose. Supplying the syntactical structures, "other kinds of," or "fruits-not-apples" is helpful once the child has the notion of combining classes and taking them apart. However, the reader must remember Piaget's admonition that it is only as the child carries out the actual operations of combining and taking apart, first physically and then mentally, that class concepts develop and that syntactical training without operational training is premature and ineffective.

4. *Taking the whole class apart to find subclasses, and making comparisons of "all" and "some"*

The test for this particular classification skill is one to which adults object. The task used in Geneva to assess development involves a set of beads, 18 of which are yellow and 2 of which are red. All the beads are made of wood. Here are the directions:

CLASS INCLUSION: ALL-SOME RELATIONS
Material:
A box with 18 wooden beads colored yellow and 2 colored red.
Presentation:
Show the box of beads to the child and ask: "What are these?" "Do you think all the yellow beads are of wood? Do you think the red beads are wood?"
Part I:
"In this box, would you say that there are more yellow beads or are there more beads made of wood?"
Justification: "Why? How do you know?"
Part II:
"There are two little girls who would like to make necklaces out of these beads. One would like first to make a necklace out of the yellow beads, and then, when she gives the beads back to me, the other girl would like to use the wooden beads. Which of the two necklaces will be the longer?"
Justification: "Why? How do you know?"
Part III:
   a) "If you give me all the yellow beads, what will be left in the box?"
   b) "If you give me all the wooden beads, will there be any beads left in the box?"
Justification: "Why? How do you know?"
Part IV:
   Repeat *Part I*

In responding to the task, children at the pre-operational level will say that there are "more yellow beads (than wooden) because there are only two red." Adults interpret this wrong response (which, incidentally, some adults will impetuously give in answer to the question but then just as quickly correct themselves when they remember that the question is asking them to compare *wooden* with *yellow*) as indicating that the *language* confuses the child, and that the task "tricks" the child. Actually, one can go back over the terms used in the problem with the child to make sure each is perfectly understood; the child will agree that *some* beads are yellow and *some* are red; that there are more yellow than red; and that *all* of the beads are made of wood. But he will respond again when asked that there are "more yellow (than wooden) because only two are red."

The reader must bear in mind that one of the characteristics of the pre-operational child is that of making judgments on the basis of perception. The child is overwhelmed by the visual display of so many yellow beads. Because he is not yet making transformations upon data, because he cannot reverse a process, he fails to go back in his mind to the *whole* class of wooden beads, and to compare the whole class with a subclass, or *all* with *some*.

How can we induce development of the classification structures essential to solving such tasks? The way suggested in this program is to have children carry out many activities where they combine subclasses to make a class and break a class down into its subclasses. They can combine yellow roses and red roses and make bunches of roses and combine roses and daisies and make bunches of flowers. They answer questions about the classes that they make: Are all of the roses yellow? Are all of the yellow flowers roses? Are there more daisies or more white daisies? Are there more roses or more flowers? Suppose all the flowers died, would there be any roses left? Such questions force the child to think about groupings that he is composing, to make comparisons between classes, and to break classes down into subgroups. As the child carries out directions for forming various subclasses and classes, the teacher calls upon him to explain what he is doing and to justify his actions, with the teacher supplying language models when they are needed.

Note that language is combined with the actions children carry out upon the flowers. Also, materials other than flowers are used in follow-up activities, so that the principle of *variety*, deemed essential to generalization and transfer, is provided for. There is memory training also. At first, children have the physical prop of flowers or other material to look at. Then they are encouraged to make a picture in their minds of how the flowers looked to begin with and, in the next step, to draw pictures of the combining, taking-apart processes. And finally, the children are asked to solve similar problems verbally, which requires that they keep the necessary comparisons in mind. The procedure here, as with procedures for developing other classification skills, follows the steps outlined by Bruner, *et al.* (1966), enactive, ikonic, symbolic. In other words, the child first carries out a transaction manually, involving the sensorimotor system; then he deals with images both mental and pictorial; then he deals with the phenomenon in words, requiring memory of the significant facts.

5. *Abstracting the common property of a class and extending the class to include all objects possessing that property*

The set of activities to develop the skills of "intension" (abstracting the common property) and extension involve also hindsight and foresight, memory and prediction. Given a collection of miniature objects—people, eating utensils, houses of various types—and three boxes into which to place objects alike in some way, and required, furthermore, to use all the objects, the child must both abstract the common property, and then, remembering that property, discover it in each object that he puts into a particular class. He must be able to look back at what he started with, and to look ahead at the same time.

Such behavior is very different from that of the younger child (3-4 years). As Inhelder and Piaget (1964) point out, children at an earlier stage do not arrange elements in collections and subcollections on the basis of similarity alone. They are unable to overlook the spatial configuration of the objects and what they do is unite them in "graphic" collections:

> The term "graphic collection" will therefore be used to describe a spatial arrangement of the elements to be classified where it seems clear that such a configuration plays an essential part in the eyes of the subject. In other words, the child is clearly unable to divorce properties (common to all members of a given class) or (properties common to some members of a class) from the graphic arrangement which he produces. Thus he may place a triangle above a square, because he thinks these two forms must be somehow related. The triangle reminds him of the roof of a house while the square can be the main part of the building. To him, this means that the triangle must be placed over the square and nowhere else. Here the spatial configuration plays an essential part in determining the intensive properties of the arrangement. Sometimes, however, we find that children use the words "some" and "all" in different ways, depending on the spatial arrangement of the parts of a collection. Here the arrangement is crucial to the determination of extensive properties. (p. 18)

Such graphic collections may take the form of laying objects in line, or making a geometrical figure or pattern out of them, or making a pretend "picture" out of them. Thus, given a set of circles, squares and triangles, the child may place a triangle on top of a square to make a house with a roof top, because "they go together to make a house," instead of abstracting the common property of squareness or triangularity or roundness out of the figures.

At the next stage in classification, the child is capable of spontaneous anticipation, even if it is imperfect. He may be unable to foresee the details of a classification, but he is no longer operating on the basis of perception. One object may strike his fancy in a particular way and he will choose the next object to go with it on the basis of a common property, although he will not be able to maintain the system for all objects. Gradually, as children have more and more experience in classifying objects, the operations of hindsight and foresight appear.

In addition to the special activities conducted in the structured periods, there are many opportunities during the preschool day for the teacher to stimulate actions upon classes and relations between classes. In the housekeeping corner, the teacher may begin by naming the common property: "Put all the things-to-eat-with, or eating utensils, on this shelf." Later, however, she may say, "Let's put all the play clothes in separate boxes. Here are three boxes. Put the clothes that are like each other, that go together in some way, in each box." Note that there may be several schemes for classifying the clothes—by color, by category, by material—*provided* the child adheres to the rule of classifying *all* the clothes. In fact, the teacher might call attention to the various classification schemes developed by different children, and encourage flexibility in changing from one criterion to another.

6. *Finding an object to fit the intersection of two classes*

Finding an object to fit the intersection of two classes is a skill that depends upon a skill developed earlier in the classification sequence, namely, abstracting the common property in a group of objects. The task used in Geneva involves pictures of a red leaf, a brown leaf, a green leaf, a purple leaf and a yellow leaf, all lined up in a horizontal row. In the vertical row are pictures of a green hat, a green jacket, a green dress, a green book and a green umbrella. The child is asked to choose from a group of pictures the one to put in a blank space where horizontal and vertical rows meet, that will "go" with both sets of objects. The group of pictures from which the child must choose includes pictures of all of the objects listed above. To solve the puzzle, the child must abstract the common property from the objects in both the vertical and the horizontal rows, keep each property in mind, and find the picture of an object that contains both properties simultaneously. Since the common property of the horizontal row is leaf-ness, and the common property of the vertical row is green-ness, he must search for a green leaf to put in the intersection of the two classes. The activity demands, then, abstracting ability, memory, and the concept of simultaneous membership in two or more classes. Earlier training experiences in this program have attempted to build these. Here, there is the opportunity to apply all three mental processes to the problem of finding an object to satisfy several conditions simultaneously, and setting off the object by means of a Venn diagram (named for the mathematician).

The equipment needed for each child consists of two nylon rope rings and colored geometric shapes. The first step in the activity requires that each child arrange the rings so that a green square is in neither ring, and then inside one ring, and finally inside both rings. The first two directions are carried out without difficulty; even the third, inside *both* rings, is carried out with considerable success. Children quickly catch on to the fact that they can put the figure inside both rings by putting one ring on top of the other. Then the teacher asks, "Can you find another way to put the figure inside both rings?" Gradually, children come to see that they can slide one of the rings to one side, more and more, until there is barely room enough in the intersection for the figure. Then more figures are introduced until, finally, there are several miscellaneous red figures in one circle and several squares of various colors in the other, and the problem is to determine which of the remaining blocks will fit in the intersection. The activity can be carried out with a variety of materials, including those used in other activities in this program. An outcome of the activity is the child's awareness that whatever he puts in the intersection must satisfy conditions of both sets of objects, and an awareness that the object in the intersection belongs to both sets, regardless of how small the intersection is.

7-8. *Making all possible combinations of elements*

The two final sets in the classification series involve combinatorial problems. Given a certain number of elements, how many combinations can you make? The high school student meets such problems, and also permutation problems, in algebra when he is asked to find all possible arrangements of three elements, *a b c*. He can make *acb, bac, bca, cab, cba*, for a total of 6 different combinations. If he has an unlimited supply of each element, that is, a quantity of *a*'s, *b*'s and *c*'s, he can, of course, etc., etc. It comes as a surprise to many high school students that the number of combina-

The materials pictured above are designed to provide practice in combining objects from different sets to form new classes. The question is, given two sets of two objects each, how many different combinations can one make? Or, specifically, if a girl has two sweaters and two skirts, how many different outfits will she be able to wear? Combining variables, keeping track of the combinations, and knowing when all possible combinations have been made are important logical operations to which children are introduced here.

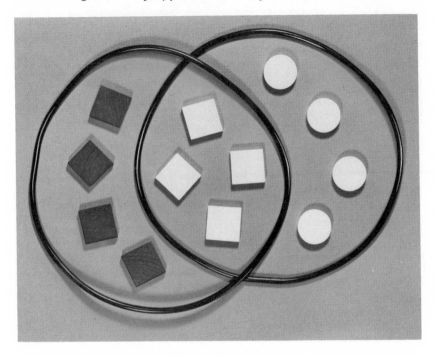

The rings permit the child to set off a class of objects, like the squares in one ring and the red figures in another, with a definite physical boundary. In successive steps, he is led to impose one ring upon another, so that there is an area of overlap. What can be put in this intersection? He must first figure out the common property of each class (above, square-ness and red-ness) and then decide which figure contains both of these properties (the red squares). Young children enjoy this challenge which utilizes ability to abstract the common property of a class, and which also fosters awareness that an object in the intersection of two sets must contain the common property of both sets.

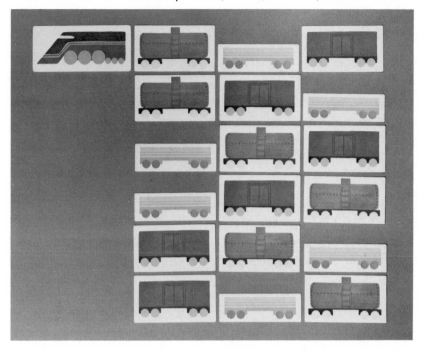

The materials shown above also provide practice in combining objects from different sets to form new classes. In this activity, the child is asked to put together as many different train-car combinations to go with the locomotive as possible, with each combination made up of a tank car, a flat car and a box car.

tions is limited, and that it is possible to make many more combinations, including *aaa, bbb, ccc, abb, bba,* and predict, in advance, what the number of combinations will be. Arranging and rearranging elements abstractly are mental transformations that are possible because of concrete operations the child has carried on at an earlier stage. A little girl who has two different skirts and two different sweaters may discover that she can make a total of four outfits, while a little boy who has one engine and three different kinds of freight cars, with several of each kind, may discover that he can make nine different arrangements of trains of two cars each.

Note that the child *may* make such discoveries. As we have pointed out earlier, children vary considerably in their level of logical development. What the child gets out of a particular experience depends in part upon what he brings to it. But it also depends upon the teacher's role of problem-maker, upon her ability to raise pertinent questions that will lead to fresh insights on the child's part.

Equipment for the first of the two combinatorial problems consists of a paper doll, plus two skirts in red and yellow and two sweaters in red and yellow. The child is first asked to name the different outfits or ways of dressing the doll that are possible with the sweaters and skirts provided. Most five-year-olds will say "two." With the equipment provided, they can discover for themselves that four combinations of two elements each are possible. They continue with trains and with additional equipment, in each case discovering the number of combinations for themselves. After combining elements in various ways, out of the action of arranging the elements, they arrive at a solution of having each element go with itself once and with each of the other elements once, and repeat this procedure for as many times as there are elements. While young children do not arrive at the generalization or law for combining elements, they are able to solve combinatorial and permutation problems by carrying out actions upon actual objects.

Combining elements so as to test all possible combinations is a mental process that adults need every day in problem solving. A door is difficult to open; we state certain propositions to explain the cause: we're turning the key too far; we aren't turning the key far enough; the door needs to be pulled toward one while the key is being turned; the door needs a kick after the key is turned. The solution might depend upon one of these factors, or upon a combination of two of them. How many possible combinations are there? Or, consider a university student working on a research problem in child development. He wants to find out what factors correlate with a particular behavior. Is it sex of the child, social class or age, or a combination of two of these? How many statistical tests must he perform to make sure of testing all variables and combinations of variables? The solution to such problems has its crude beginnings in the combinations children are asked to make in these activities.

We have just described the mental processes involved in classification that develop in early childhood. Classification structures are not completed by age seven, but, as Inhelder and Piaget have shown, the groundwork is laid during the pre- and primary school years. Special training on the processes, combined with reinforcement during play activities, will hopefully result in more children being capable of logical thinking, and thus more successful, in acquiring new concepts.

Herb Weitman, University City Public Schools, University City, Missouri

The picture above shows a child working to solve a conservation of length problem. Does the child recognize that, in order to build a "tower" as tall as the one pictured, he must compensate for the fact that the one-piece tower is built on a higher base? The problem is also a measurement problem; to be sure the two "towers" are equal in height, the child must be able to use each dowel rod as a unit, applying it more than once, if necessary.

5. *Development of Number, Measurement and Space Operations*

INTRODUCING YOUNG CHILDREN to mathematics is not a new idea in early childhood education; it has long been common practice in kindergartens and nursery schools to teach children to count and to distribute materials on a one-to-one basis. But, as with classification, the researches of the Geneva school have given us insight into the mental processes involved in the development of space and number concepts which, in turn, have raised questions about the value of traditional practices and have provided the foundation for a fresh approach to a preschool mathematics curriculum.

THE DEVELOPMENT OF NUMBER CONCEPTS

Piaget and his co-workers have been interested in finding out how mathematical notions emerge in the thought of the child. Using the clinical method, the Geneva school has presented to children between four and eight years of age tasks which would reveal their underlying assumptions about the nature of number, measurement and space. Piaget has not been interested in number readiness as defined by arithmetic readiness tests but, rather, in children's awareness of the fundamental properties of number, measurement and space. For example, his primary concern is not with whether or not the child can add 8+8 but whether or not the child understands that a group of eight objects continues to be equal in number to a second group of eight objects, even with a transformation in the space occupied by the objects. For example, one can line up 8 dolls in a row and ask a child to take out from a group of 10 chairs enough chairs so that each doll has one to sit on. Most four- and five-year-olds do this, lining up a row of chairs with each chair placed at the feet of a doll (children are told not to seat the dolls). However, some who lack visual correspondence will not stop at the eighth chair but will continue to give out chairs until all are exhausted. With the child who is successful at Step 1, the experimenter next pushes the dolls together in a heap and asks the child if there are still as many chairs as dolls, one chair for each doll, or if there are more chairs or more dolls. The child who cannot conserve, who judges on the basis of how things look, will affirm that there are more chairs, because "they're spread out and the dolls are close together."

Interestingly enough, counting does not help; the child may count 8 dolls and 8 chairs, but still say that there are more chairs if the dolls are bunched together, even though he also says that the number was the same before the dolls were moved. Eight does not equal 8, for the preoperational child. Number and space are confused in his mind, and number of objects changes with the amount of space the objects occupy. So does space change according to the objects occupying that space. A room becomes shorter in length when objects are placed in the space between back and front of the room.

Basic to our understanding of number, measurement and space is the notion of conservation—that number and space are conserved, remain the same in quantity, even with a transformation in appearance, provided nothing has been added or taken away. The principle of conservation, however, has a much broader application than the example given here. As Piaget uses the term, one comes to realize that conservation and rational activity are inextricably linked; he points out (1952a) that conservation is a necessary condition of all experience and reasoning; that we can acquire concepts only when we recognize that they require a certain permanence in their definition; that certain properties retain their identity or are conserved in spite of an apparent change. Thus the acquisition of all concepts is possible only when the child can conserve.

Two fundamental notions involved in number are *cardination* and *ordination*. In order to develop a concept of number, the child must understand that number is a class. The cardinal value of a class of 10 objects is 10. This is its invariant property, a property that is conserved across changes in appearance. When we talk about a class of 10 objects, we are, in effect, treating the objects as if they were all alike; we disregard object differences as well as object arrangements.

But number is not simply a class. In order to arrive at the *name* of the class (which is its cardinal value) we must count the objects one by one. The order in which we count makes no difference, but there must be an order so that we don't count an object twice. When order is considered, the objects counted *are* different from one another. They differ in ordinal position: first object counted, second object counted, etc. Thus, number has an ordinal component as well as a cardinal one, and these two notions must be synthesized before the concept of number is logically achieved.

The study of the nature of number, then, includes both class and seriation operations. Much of what has been said in the chapter on *Classification*, and will be said in the chapter on *Seriation* to follow, actually applies to the development of number concepts as well. The notion of classes, relations, and numbers develop in a mutually dependent way; all depend upon the child's ability to conserve which, in turn, depends upon logic. The separate distinctions that we make here in the various cognitive domains, and that Piaget makes in his research, are purely arbitrary.

There is a way in which equivalence of sets can be established other than by counting, and that is by a one-to-one correspondence. This method is a mathematically certain way of establishing cardinal equivalence. *Optical* equivalence comes first. This occurs when the child recognizes equivalence by matching the objects one for one; equivalence is then apparent to the eye (by putting a spoon in a cup or lining up two rows of objects, for example). For the preoperational child, when optical equivalence is destroyed, equivalence is lost; it is only as the child can operate mentally upon the data, when he can move objects about in his mind, that he can retain equivalence in the face of a physical transformation.

For example, in the task already described, where the dolls were pushed together so that each was no longer directly opposite a chair, the child who is at the stage of concrete operations will say, "It's still the same number. Just put the dolls back the way they were and you can see there's just as many (as there are chairs)." Or, an occasional child will say, "There's still just as many. You didn't add any and you didn't take any away, so the number (of dolls and chairs) has got to be the same."

As has been pointed out in earlier chapters, logical operations develop out of the actions of the child in grouping, ordering, comparing, etc. Thought arises out of action, Piaget says over and over again. Mathematical thinking is no exception; it becomes logical as the result of actions the child performs with objects. These actions lead the child to assimilate new data which eventually transforms existing structures of thought. It becomes possible for the child to go back in thought to the starting place and to make comparisons of the state of affairs before and after a transformation has taken place; to know the circumstances under which things remain the same or change; to put bits and pieces of ideas together in different ways; to combine parts to make a whole.

A brief summary of the tasks developed at Geneva to study the development of mathematical concepts will be useful to the reader in understanding the sections to follow. The tasks include:

1. *Activities involving conservation of "continuous" and "discontinuous" quantities*

(i.e., quantities that are smooth or flow like water or clay as contrasted with quantities made up of readily apparent discrete objects like dolls, flowers, etc.) One activity ("discontinuous" quantity) involved separating a collection of beads into two similar containers, dropping a bead from each hand into each container simultaneously. After the child asserts that each container has exactly the same number of beads, one lot is then put into a tall narrow container and the child is asked if the number of beads is still the same in both containers. A similar experiment is carried out using two identical containers of water ("continuous" quantity), with the water then poured first into a tall, skinny container and next into one that is wide and shallow.

2. *Activities involving one-to-one correspondence*

The dolls-and-chairs activity already described is an example of this type of task. Other activities involve materials where there is a natural link between sets, like flowers in vases and shoes on dolls. Other activities have been used where the natural link between sets of materials is missing—a row of counters to be matched by the child from a pile of additional counters. And, as with dolls-and-chairs, the same procedure is followed of spreading out and closing up one set or the other so that each configuration is different in length from the other.

3. *Activities involving division of materials into sets of equal number*

For example, a child might be asked to arrange two unequal piles of counters so that they are equal in number, or to divide a single pile into two equal parts. Or, the child might be asked about the equality of a group of eight sweets divided into two parts of four each to be eaten in the morning and afternoon of one day, as compared with a group divided into two parts of one and seven to be eaten on the next day. Although the sweets came from sets equal in number, the division produces inequality in the preoperational child's mind.

The developmental stages in the acquisition of number concepts are essentially the same as for the acquisition of other concepts. Initially, the preoperational child denies conservation. Whether the task is one involving division into sets or pouring a quantity into containers of different shapes, the child judges in terms of how things look to him. Since he does not yet consider two variables or two dimensions at once, he decides on equality of two sets of objects or two quantities of matter on the basis of the particular variable or dimension that is most prominent perceptually. This may be the height of a liquid in a container: "This one (the tall, narrow container) has more because it (the 'lemonade') goes up higher (than it does in the standard container)."

The preoperational stage is followed by a transition stage where the child is likely to achieve conservation under conditions of minimum transformation of perceptual data. That is, if the dolls are not spread out *too* far, or if the container into which the "lemonade" is poured is not *too* different in height, then the child can maintain conservation. He loses it, however, and reverts to non-conservation responses with no indication of logical operations when the visual display is sufficiently changed.

Eventually, for most children at six or seven years of age, the stage of concrete-operational thought is achieved. The responses of the child to the tasks described become more logical. Conservation of number on one-to-one correspondence tasks appears first; conservation of quantity (amount of "stuff" in balls of clay, or amount of "lemonade") is next; typically, children can conserve number by five or six years of age and by six or seven, they can conserve quantity. Conservation of other variables, such as length, weight and volume, follow at eight, nine and ten years of age, approximately.

THE TRAINING PROGRAM: NUMBER

To help children acquire concepts of one-to-one correspondence, many experiences in which children operate upon a variety of materials are necessary. In the Piagetian curriculum we have been describing, activities involving the purchase of materials at a store, one penny for one item, or the exchange of objects, on a one-for-one basis, are employed. In each case, the procedure is essentially the same: for the first step, a physical correspondence is established between an object in one set and an object in a second set. To build the notion of correspondence at the physical level, sets of objects that fit together in some natural way can be used: dolls and chairs, or flowers in vases. Also helpful is the actual physical exchange of objects. One child has a set of objects and the other a set of pennies. First, each child takes turns at being the buyer.

The teacher is the storekeeper. Every time the child buys a package from the "storekeeper," he must pay one penny. When he runs out of money, the teacher asks him if the number of pennies she has and the number cf packages he has are the same. The game is made harder by having more packages than pennies. Or, the teacher may stop the game after five exchanges and ask, "Can you tell me how many pennies I have left? How do you know how many I have left?"

Once physical correspondence has been achieved, the teacher can then proceed to work on the problem of conservation of number after physical correspondence has been destroyed. Training techniques are based on findings of what factors seem to be effective in including logical operations (see papers by Wohlwill (1960), Smedslund (1961a, b), Kohnstamm (1967), Smith (1968)). Introducing a transformation in one set of materials *very gradually* is one such technique. The set of pennies can be shifted, as the child watches, from a straight line to a slight curve and from a slight curve, by almost imperceptible steps, to a semicircle. With successive transformations there comes a point where the visual display changes sufficiently so that the child loses conservation. However, after repeated trials and with a variety of activities, it dawns on the child that "It doesn't matter how you spread them around. If you started the same, then you've still got the same."

The procedure of adding an object to one of two sets the child has found to be equivalent in number and asking him if each set still has the same number of objects is also useful in developing the concept that number does not change unless something is added to, or taken away from a set. An effective activity can be done with one-inch cubes of two different colors. The child is asked to imagine that each cube is a cupcake and to make two identical rows of six cupcakes each. He has six pipe cleaners and can establish physical correspondence by stretching a pipe cleaner between a blue cake and a red cake in each row. Then the blue row is shifted around, but always in such a way that the pipe cleaner can still be placed between matching cakes. The teacher adds a "cake" or takes one away as the rows are pushed farther apart and asks about the equivalence of two sets and, also, for a justification of the response. Again, language is important; the teacher asks over and over again,

"If we add something, what happens?" (The row gets longer; there are more); "If we take away something, what happens?" (There are less; not as many.)

A very simple but effective training device employs quantities of colored beads, two plastic 8 oz. containers, one low and broad and the other tall and skinny, and some brown paper sacks. The child drops a bead from each hand into each of the containers at the same time, sometimes chanting as he does so, "one in here; one in here." From time to time, brown paper sacks with a hole in the center are put over the containers and the procedure is repeated. Children deny that both containers have the same amount of beads when they can see the beads, but invariably give conservation responses when they cannot perceive the inequality of the level of beads in the containers, and eventually the discrepancy between the responses they give in the two situations becomes apparent to them, and they say excitedly, "It's got to be the same; I put the same in each jar. It doesn't matter how it looks." Operational structures are obviously emerging.

Since the notion of conservation is basic to the development of number concepts, we also include training for conservation of quantity. The activity involved is water pouring; will the quantity of water remain the same when poured into a container different in shape? We start with two 8 oz. beakers almost filled with water. The children pour back and forth until they are satisfied that each beaker has exactly the same amount of water. Then one beaker is emptied into two 4 oz. beakers, almost filling them. Or, one of the original beakers might be poured into a tall, skinny container, or a flat, broad container, filling each to the brim. The children are queried in each case about whether quantity remains the same after pouring as in the beaker that has not been emptied.

Since the preoperational child does not coordinate the change in one dimension with a change in the other, he will think that the two smaller glasses contain more "because there are two," or that the flat container or the tall one has more "because it's full all the way up." Many experiences in pouring water from a container of one shape to another, and *reversing the process,* and in describing the containers in two dimensions (the container is taller but thinner) lead eventually to operations of reversibility and logical multiplication (i.e., recognizing that a change in one dimension is compensated for by a change in another). At this stage, no doubt remains in the child's mind; he is absolutely certain of the equality of liquid regardless of what container it is in. Furthermore, his responses clearly reveal that he is transforming what he sees by means of mental operations. He says, typically, "They're the same. Just pour the four glasses back, and you'll see they're the same." (Reversibility: reversing the act of pouring.) "They've got to be the same. The tall one makes up for being taller by being skinnier." (Associativity: compensating by breaking down the whole into parts and rearranging the parts.) "They're the same. You didn't add any and you didn't take any away, so they've got to be the same." (Identity: adding nothing and taking nothing away doesn't change anything.)

The Development of Concepts of Measurement

The reader may think of measurement in terms of applying a foot ruler to a length to be measured, or of putting an object on a scale and reading off a number from the scale, or of using some other instrument marked off in standard units. However, each standard unit has a long history in man's past, and it is the rediscovery by the child of the need first for a unit and eventually for a standard unit that concerns Piaget. Measuring involves first and foremost a change of position which may be effected by the moving eye comparing distant objects, or the movement may be that of a common unit of measure which links distant objects together. In fact, essential to measuring is the notion of unit-iteration, of deciding upon a unit and repeating it.

The task developed at Geneva to reveal concepts of measurement is one where the child is asked to compose out of blocks of different sizes a "tower" equal in height to another "tower" already built. However, the second tower is to be built on another table lower or higher than the first Piaget (1953a), describes what happens:

> Children's attempts to deal with this problem go through a fascinating evolution. The youngest children build up the second tower to the same visual level as the first, without worrying

about the difference in height of the tables. They compare the towers by stepping back and sighting them. At a slightly more advanced stage a child lays a long rod across the tops of the two towers to make sure that they are level. Somewhat later he notices that the base of his tower is not at the same level as the model's. He then wants to place his tower next to the model on the same table to compare them. Reminded that the rules of the game forbid him to move his tower, he begins to look around for a measuring standard. Interestingly enough, the first that comes to his mind is his own body. He puts one hand on top of his tower and the other at its base, and then, trying to keep his hands the same distance apart, he moves over to the other tower to compare it. Children of about the age of six often carry out this work in a most assured manner, as if their hands could not change position on the way! Soon they discover that the method is not reliable, and then they resort to reference points on the body. The child will line up his shoulder with the top of his tower, mark the spot opposite the base on his thigh with his hand and walk over to the model to see whether the distance is the same.

Eventually the idea of an independent measuring tool occurs to the child. His first attempt in this direction is likely to be the building of a third tower next to and the same height as the one he has already erected. Having built it, he moves it over to the first table and matches it against the model; this is allowed by the rules. The child's arrival at this stage presupposes a process of logical reasoning. If we call the model tower A, the second tower C and the movable tower B, the child has reasoned that $B = C$ and $B = A$, therefore $A = C$. (pp. 78-79)

The experimenter proceeds at this point to show the child three rods: one longer than, one shorter than, and one just the same height as the model tower. The child is asked whether he can use one of the rods to see if his tower is the same height as the model. At first, he thinks that the rod must be just the same length as the height of the tower, and he will place the rod alongside each to measure, although he may throw his measurement off by placing the base of the rod some distance away from the base of the tower so that the rod forms a diagonal to the tower rather than lying flat up against it. Later he conceives of the idea of using a longer rod and marking the tower height on it with his finger. Here, again, he may be inept in moving the position of his finger as he transfers the rod from one tower to another. Finally, he realizes that he can use a shorter rod and measure the height of the tower by applying the rod a certain number of times up the side. This is the beginning of true measurement.

Piaget (1953) analyzes the logic of the child's operation for us. He points out that one mental operation involved here is the process of division, which permits the child to conceive that the whole is composed of a number of parts added together. The second operation is that of substitution, which enables the child to conceive of one of the parts as a unit and to apply the unit upon other parts. Measurement develops later than does the number concept because it is more difficult to think of a whole as divided into equal parts than it is to deal with elements which are already separate.

THE TRAINING PROGRAM: MEASUREMENT

Training experiences in structured lessons are developed around tasks like constructing a "tower" in which a variety of measuring tools is used. In general, children's development appears to follow along the lines described by Piaget, with the body being used as the first measuring tool. After children discover how a hand or the height of one's chest might be used to assess equality, they are encouraged to seek out their own units of measurement. They use books, lengths of string, blocks—literally anything they can lay their hands on; they show their acquisition of the unit iteration principle in their application of invented units.

Other kinds of experiences can help to build the principle of unit iteration in areas other than measurement of length. Take, for example, the problem of conservation of liquid quantity, of trying to decide whether two containers, very different in shape, contain the same amount of liquid. One can be certain by using a unit of measurement, a smaller container, and keeping track of the number of times it must be filled to fill each of the larger containers.

In our program we first provided many experiences in pouring water from a container of one size into another and noting water level. The procedure varies from the water-pouring experiences previously described. One teacher's report of progress is as follows:

I began by showing children one small beaker and one large one. I asked them how many small cans of water it would take to fill the big one. The children guessed different numbers—2, 3, 4. I poured while they watched and discovered that two of the small ones filled one of the large. I gave them pointers on pouring. We talked about differences in dimensions—taller, shorter, wider, skinnier.

Next I asked if the water from the larger container would fit in a container (same capacity) that was broad and flat in shape.

Tony was positive that water would fit, but had no explanation. The rest of the children said "no," the dish was too small. Here the children did their own pouring. The water fit exactly. I asked if there would be just as much water to drink as before. The children said there was more in the first container. We discussed differences in dimensions again; I emphasized vocabulary. The children tried pouring back water from the flat containers, but there was much spillage. I demonstrated, and the children saw that the liquid was the "same" as before.

Work continued with the children during short periods of directed activity. A month later, the teacher reported:

June 29. We had another water pouring session. All the children except Kathy can now assess quantity if the shape of the container isn't too different. They agreed that the full 8 oz. jar had more water than the full 6 oz. one and that the 6 oz. one wouldn't fill the 8 oz. container, even though the water level was practically the same in each case. Using a small container (4 oz.) as a unit and filling containers of different sizes and shapes seems to have helped, together with work on vocabulary. Children still have not achieved conservation fully; when I try them out using containers *very* different in height, they lose the ability to conserve. The height of the water level in a tall, skinny container is still terribly misleading. Although Carla and Tony seem to be on the verge of conserving, Carla watches like a hawk each time she pours to see that no drop of water is lost. Tony also seems aware, but doesn't concentrate as well.

When the child begins to *do* something with the data, when he begins to transform what he sees by means of mental operations, he is in a transition stage, as responses of some of the children in the above protocol reveal. The child may be inconsistent; he may lose sight of conservation when the new display is very different from the original, but the teacher should be alert to such inconsistencies and changes of mind, for they usually indicate progress toward reversibility and conservation.

The Development of Concepts of Space

A professor of physics who has taught thousands of physics students has observed, only partly facetiously, that the world seems to be divided into two kinds of people: geometers and nongeometers. It is certainly true that even among the very bright there is great variability in the ability to deal with many aspects of geometry and, particularly, space relations. There are those who relate to space very well and those who find it difficult to visualize what happens even in a simple 180° transformation of an object in space. To a certain extent, and perhaps to a very great extent, such differences are due to early experiences. It may be that children who engage in many play activities involving movement in space are more likely to be competent in this area than children who busy themselves with other kinds of activities.

According to Piaget, concepts of space begin to develop in the cradle. He cites some examples: by 5 or 6 weeks of age, the young baby is capable of recognizing a familiar face, despite changes in distance or the effects of perspective. During the 4 to 10-month period, prehension and vision become coordinated, so it is possible for the infant not only to see objects in space, but to grasp what he sees within his reach. At 9 months, given a long narrow object that will not fit a narrow space when held horizontally, the child can turn the object vertically so that it relates to space in a different way. Throughout the sensorimotor period, the child explores objects, begins to abstract shapes, reckon with distance, and form images of shapes and their relationship to space.

In studying how space becomes represented in thought, Piaget has been concerned with the development of concepts of open and closed figures, of geometrical shapes, of spatial perspective, and of objects in a plane. With respect to open and closed figures, Piaget found that recognition of such properties appears before that of geometrical shapes. Children of three years were asked to match by manual exploration objects that they could not see; they could distinguish between objects open and closed (a washer and a disk, for example) before they could discriminate between a circle and a square. With respect to spatial perspective, children at the preoperational stage found it difficult to imagine how an object would appear from various points of view; for each task they were asked to do, they invariably performed it from their own perspective rather than that of another. Piaget finds this tendency to be yet another example of *egocentricism,* the tendency to see things always from one's own viewpoint and to find it impossible to assume the viewpoint of another. Finally, when it came to representing objects in a plane, as, for example, planting posts "nice and straight" on a model of a mountain and drawing the result, the preoperational child was inadequate to the task; his posts were always perpendicular to the slope of the mountain.

THE TRAINING PROGRAM: SPACE

To aid in the acquisition of space concepts, we developed a number of activities for our program. Two of these involve spatial visualization, that is, being able to visualize how something will look if it is moved in space, or how it will look from another point of view. In one, the child is shown a place setting (placement, knife, fork, spoon, glass, napkin, all correctly positioned on the mat) and asked to set a place for a friend on the opposite side of the table, with knife, fork, etc., arranged for his friend in the same way as they are for him. In the other activity, children are lined up in front of a model of a house with a garage, and a tree in front of the house. A doll is placed on the opposite side. They are asked to pick from a group of pictures the one that shows the scene as the doll sees it. The doll is placed in turn in various positions around the scene and the directions repeated.

In both instances, children's thinking is characterized by what Piaget calls *spatial egocentricism*, that is, the child sees things from his own viewpoint and cannot assume the viewpoint of another. Although he may move around the table to inspect the knife, the fork and the spoon that he has placed without any transformation, he says, "That's the same thing. The knife is the same for him as it is for me on the other side." We found in the training program that building the transformation into the sensorimotor system by carrying out an actual physical correspondence was helpful. The child was given a knife to clutch in his hand and told to walk around to the other side and put it down on the side of the plate to match the other side. Or, the child was asked to place left and right hands on fork and knife, the whole place mat was then slowly rotated by another child, while hands were kept in the same place, until a 180° transformation had been completed. Or, the child was asked to sit in front of the placemat, to raise a hand in the air, drop it slowly straight down on an eating utensil, and then with that same hand raised in air, repeat the performance on the opposite side of the table. As a result of such activities and those carried out throughout the day in natural play situations, there gradually emerged a realization that things will look different according to the position of the observer and that left-right positions will be reversed under the circumstances described. While the concept of relativity will still be incomplete, children can, with training, develop a genuine feeling for spatial transformations and will abandon egocentricism.

The second set of activities to develop spatial visualization revolved around a tableau, consisting of a house, a separate garage, and a tree standing in front of the house. Involved here are not only transformations of left and right, but also of "in front of" and "in back of." Seen from the child's point of view, the garage is on the right and the tree is in front of the house. From the doll's point of view, objects are reversed. In response to the question of which picture shows what the doll would see from the other side, children will typically begin by choosing a picture on the basis of a dominant feature. Color stands out for some, and they will say,

Many adults have difficulty in picturing how a particular scene will look from a different viewpoint. Young children in particular, as Piaget has pointed out, tend to have an egocentric point of view which makes it difficult for them to take on the viewpoint of another. The materials shown are designed to provide training in relativity of perspective. The child views the scene always from the same position. The doll moves around from one side of the setting to another. The child must choose from pictures of the setting taken from different positions the one which corresponds to the view the doll sees.

Here are two grassy parking lots, each exactly the same size as the other. Suppose twelve cars are parked on the grass in one lot, lined up next to one another in two neat rows. Suppose twelve cars are parked on the grass in the other lot, but spread out in random fashion. Would there be as much grass to mow in the one field as in the other? To solve the problem, the child must realize that one can put parts together in different ways to form a whole, but that as long as nothing is added and nothing is taken away, both number and area remain the same.

"This one. Because there's a blue roof in the picture and the house has a blue roof, too." For others, however, the tree is the dominant feature; they will select one of the views showing the tree, even though the view is from the side, and justify their choice on the basis of "It's got a tree, and there's a tree here, too." Concepts of "in front of" and "in back of" elude them; they judge what the doll will see in terms of what *they* see and fail to realize that from the opposite side of where they sit, the tree is no longer "in front of" the house, but is, indeed, "in back of" it.

The first step in developing the notion of relativity of perspective where both left-right and front-back transformations were involved, was to free the child from the *egocentric* point of view that regardless of where an observer is stationed, the observer sees things as the child does. Playing a game with another child in which each sat at opposite sides of the tableau and chose a picture to represent what *he* thought the other person was seeing proved to be a useful first step. It is not at all uncommon for a child to see what he wants to see, and if he is sent around the table to look at the tableau from the opposite side, to continue to adhere to his choice of picture which represented the view of the tableau *before* a transformation. However, with a peer sitting across the table telling him what he (the peer) thinks the first child is seeing (which *isn't* what he is seeing, but is, rather, the peer's view), the child's strong belief is shattered and he becomes ready to consider that the view from the other side may be different. Some psychologists talk about the necessity for "cognitive dissonance" to upset previously held beliefs, feedback from one's peers which is dissonant to what one has believed is more likely to be effective than contrary evidence available to the senses. Once the egocentric point of view has been effectively challenged, the child is more receptive to other cues that will aid development of left-right and front-back transformations.

There is a third kind of activity developed for the program, one to induce the concepts of a system of reference to position objects in space. By a system of reference for organizing space, Piaget refers to concepts of the vertical and horizontal which are used in making judgments about objects in space. When we hang a picture on the wall, how do we know whether or not it is "straight"?

We line it up mentally with horizontal and vertical lines in the room and reach a decision. How do we "know" that a post or stake we are putting in the ground is straight? We unconsciously compare it with the position of our own bodies or with other upright objects in the same subspace. As Piaget (1956) says,

> As adults we are so accustomed to using a system of reference and organizing our empirical space by means of coordinate axes which appear self-evident (like the vertical provided by the plumb-line and the horizontal given by a water level), that it may seem absurd to ask at what age the child acquires these ideas. It will be said that as a result of lying flat on his back the child is aware of the horizontal right from the cradle, and that he discovers the vertical as soon as he attempts to raise himself. The postural system would thus appear to provide a ready-made coordinate space, the organs of equilibrium with their only too-well-known semicircular canals solving the entire problem. In which case it would indeed appear odd to want to raise the problem all over again with the 4 to 10 year old child!
>
> Here we touch on one of the worst misconceptions which has plagued the theory of geometrical concepts. From the fact that the child breathes, digests and possesses a heart that beats we do not conclude that he has any idea of alimentary metabolism or the circulatory system. At the very most he may have noticed his movements in breathing, or felt his pulse. But such perceptual-motor awareness does not lead to any understanding of the internal phenomena of which these movements are only the outward and visible sign. Similarly, from the fact that he can stand up or lie flat, the child at first derives only a strictly empirical awareness of the two postures and nothing more. To superimpose upon this a more general schema he must at some point go outside the purely postural field and compare his own position with those of surrounding objects, and this is something beyond purely empirical knowledge. (p. 378)

That the young child cannot go outside "the purely postural field and compare his own position with that of surrounding objects" is obvious from his drawings. Between 4 and 8 years, the child puts chimneys perpendicular to sloping roofs and even at right-angles to hills they are supposed to be climbing. While they represent the vertical axis correctly, there is a total disregard of the horizontal axis. What the child needs to develop is a system of reference to include two coordinates: a horizontal axis *and* a vertical axis, to consider both of these together, and to judge transformations in space within the framework of such a coordinate system.

In our Piagetian curriculum, we concentrate on the development of such a coordinate system. We can adapt one of the Geneva tasks involving the water surface in a tilted bottle. How does the child "see" water level when the bottle is tilted? His drawings of the result show that water level is pictured as horizontal to the base of the container, and not level with the table top or the horizon. Although the child is actually *looking* at the water level as he draws, he draws the level as tilted.

Now it is strange that the child disregards the horizontal reference points (like the table top) available to him. In fact, it is strange that he errs at all, for he is surrounded in the physical world by a natural reference frame. As Piaget (1956) points out,

> On the empirical level, the horizontal is given by the plane on which everyday objects rest, the earth itself (where flat), or the artificial planes of floors, terraces, and so on. Another important factor is the surface of a liquid, which for little children living in Geneva is illustrated daily by the surface of Lake Leman, to say nothing of the levels of drinks in cups and glasses. As for the vertical axis, this is provided by the walls of rooms and houses, by posts, chimney stacks, trees, and so on. (p. 379)

Some four-year-olds are incapable of representing planes at all. Instead of drawing the water as a plane surface, they show the water in a ball in the center of the flask—and this while they are looking at the actual container. Those more advanced show water level as a plane surface, but when the bottle is tilted, they show water level as tilted, also.

As Piaget points out, children look at containers of liquid all of their lives and never see what they draw. One reasonable explanation in keeping with what we know about the preoperational child is that the child draws the water as level with the *nearest* horizontal—the top or bottom of the container—rather than with the table top. Training, therefore, should concentrate on helping the child move away from a judgment based upon proximity, to a judgment based upon a relatively stable horizontal, like table top or floor. The mental operation here involves coordinating two variables, vertical and horizontal, into a single reference frame. The principle to follow is to *decenter* the child's reference point, the tilted side of the bottle, and to substitute for it two reference points: table top or floor, and wall. In each case, the substitutes can be made to stand out by the use of vivid colors and proximity.

Some of the techniques that can be used to foster development of ability first to recognize and then to coordinate the two variables, horizontal and vertical, are as follows:

1. In the water level activity, place a brightly colored cardboard over the bottle, parallel to the water level and *close to it* in such a way that the lower tilted side of the bottle is obscured. Children then draw water level and cardboard. They can compare these drawings with their previous drawings where water level was shown as tilted.

2. Gradually move the cardboard lower and lower down, making a gradual transformation, until children are able to use the table top as a basis of comparison.

3. Set up a slanting walking board near a classroom wall (any plank with one end set on a raised surface like a block or chair will do). The floor and wall should be made to stand out perceptually by putting down brightly colored strips of paper horizontally and vertically near the walking board. One child (a doll can be used if the plank is not strong enough for a child) can walk or be walked half way up the plank. The child or doll should be very close to the colored strip on the wall. Children can observe the child or doll in reference to the floor and in reference to the wall; they can draw lines for the floor and wall, and then draw the child as if he were "magic" and able to stand in the air without support.

4. Children can draw a mountain on a sheet of drawing paper, 9" x 12". They can color a narrow strip along the vertical edge and another strip of a different color along the horizontal edge of the paper. They can use toothpicks of the same color as the vertical edge to represent human figures. They can then place the "men"

as if they were climbing the "mountain," using the colored vertical edge as a guide.

As with other directed activities in the Piagetian curriculum, there are many opportunities throughout the day for the teacher to reinforce the learnings in the structured sessions. Some children have to begin at the level of representing water in a horizontal plane instead of in little balls inside the bottle. Experiences in filling containers with colorless water and showing on the drawings a line for water level only, rather than drawing a colored liquid inside the bottle, are helpful here.

Making a vertical and horizontal reference point external to the jar perceptually vivid through proximity and color is an effective first step in moving the child toward the more abstract notions of vertical and horizontal. One child in our program made sufficient progress by year's end (kindergarten) that he was able to answer correctly the teacher's question as to what would happen to water level if the whole table were tilted or the floor on which the table was resting was tilted. In each case the child was able to find a reference point outside the system itself and to orient objects in space by means of a coordinate system.

LANGUAGE TRAINING AND MATHEMATICAL THINKING

The structured activities in connection with number, measurement and space lend themselves nicely to language training. Both vocabulary and syntactical training can be included in the lessons. Here are examples of vocabulary included in connection with the training in certain logical concepts already described:

1. *Conservation of Number*
   Vocabulary for comparing quantity: *more, less, the same, as many as, before, after.*
2. *Conservation of Liquid Quantity*
   Vocabulary to describe dimensions of size: *tall, short, skinny, fat, wide, narrow, high, low.*
   Number names to 5 with one-to-one correspondence.
3. *Conservation of Surface Area*
   Vocabulary of transformations: *Line them up the same way, some other way, before, after, the same as, more, not as much.*

3. *Conservation of Length*
   Vocabulary for comparing length and position: *taller than, higher than, shorter than, the same length as, on top of, under, along side of, near, close to, up against.*
5. *Relativity of Position*
   Vocabulary for describing position: *across from, opposite, the same side, the other side, left, right, in back of, in front of.*
6. *Reference System for Organizing Space*
   Vocabulary for describing water level: *level with* or *leveled, tilt* or *tilted, line up with* or *lined up with.*

It is safe to say that most teachers of young children spend some time either formally or informally teaching children to count, to make one-one correspondences, to "read" a calendar and to do other number-related activities. Probably far fewer teachers have thought of including measurement and space concepts in the pre-school curriculum. Yet, training experiences in these two important areas can contribute much to children's mathematical thinking. Conducting the training sessions and listening to children's responses will make teachers more alert to opportunities in children's play to reinforce measurement and space concepts.

Herb Weitman, University City Public Schools, University City, Missouri

Children work with geometric shapes, arranging them in order of size. The mental operations involved in this activity are identifying variables of size and shape and keeping relations of size and shape in mind when seriating. You will find two general tendencies in solving the problem of identifying variables of size and shape that are characteristic of the pre-operational child: he works in trial-and-error fashion with no anticipatory scheme in mind, and he has difficulty in keeping both criteria in mind at the same time. Thus, he will seriate according to one criterion, and he will switch from one to another.

6. Development of
Seriation Operations

In ADDITION to classifying, there is another way in which the young child gradually systematizes his world, and that is by establishing relations *between* objects, by arranging them in some kind of order. Piaget gives the name *seriation* to this operation. In seriating, the child looks for differences; a series is really a chain of differences. The differences may be in size, color, intensity or other properties that can be detected visually, or they may be temporal in nature and involve events that happen at different time intervals. In any event, in seriating, the child imposes some kind of order upon objects or events and eventually becomes aware of generalizations or laws implicit in the order.

At the simplest level, ordering may simply mean designating the order in which objects or events will be arranged: alphabetical order, as in dictionaries and encyclopedias, or chronological order, as in the calendar, for example. Here, the differences involve position or time. But even at this very elementary level, there are certain logical principles which govern the relationship. If we know, for example, that A comes before B and B before C, then A, therefore, also comes before C.

Also, if we are given the problem, "Jimmy runs faster than Tony; Jimmy runs more slowly than Mark. Who runs the fastest?" we know that the solution depends upon arranging all the items in the series according to the same property of being fast. We change the statement, therefore, to read, "Jimmy runs faster than Tony; Mark runs faster than Jimmy; therefore Mark is the fastest runner and Tony is the slowest." When we order a series, we know logically that we must arrange items so that we are making comparisons along the same dimension.

At a complex level, we can find examples of seriation where the principle is more involved than in an alphabetical or chronological one. In chemistry, for example, elements are ordered according to the number of protons (or electrons) in the nucleus of the atom; man's search for regularity has led him to discover this basis for ordering which, in turn, helps to unravel chemical mysteries. The periodic table is another way of ordering elements; it groups them according to certain properties. The table is like a calendar with elements having similar properties in the same column. Very inert gases like helium, for example, are grouped in one family in a vertical column, just like the Mondays on a calendar. Seriating along the horizontal is in terms of days of the week on the calendar; in the periodic table, it is in terms of atomic number.

In Piagetian theory, more complex structures are based upon the simpler ones, and ordering a series of objects or events is often the first step leading to more difficult manipulations. Take, for example, a permutations problem which is one of the Piaget tasks administered to children in the intermediate grades. In this task, the subject is asked to decide how many combinations of two-digit numbers he can make with the digits 1 and 2. The answer is "four"; he can make 11, 12, 21, 22. Next, he is asked how many two-digit numbers he can make with 3 digits, 1, 2, and 3. The answer is "nine"; he can make 11, 12, 13, 21, 22, 23, 31, 32, 33. He is asked, in turn, to answer with respect to 4 and 5 digits, and to predict in advance of laying out the squares of cardboard with digits printed on them how many he can make. It is interesting to note that the child who approaches success with the problem is the child who first arranges the numbers in some kind of series. Note the order in laying out the series in the above.

Still a different kind of task in which seriation represents a first step is the one involving indirect proportion. The child in intermediate grades is asked to find the numbered spot on one arm of a two-pan balance where he can place a weight weighing 6 oz. to balance a 3 oz. weight in the number 4 position on the other arm of the balance. Children may first try seriating by trial and error. They begin by putting the 6 oz. weight at the number 4 position and note that it is much too heavy. They then "inch" in toward the fulcrum a notch at a time until the balance is in equilibrium. After such "inching" operations, which is seriating in a concrete-operational way, it may occur to the subject that there is a way of predicting in advance where the weight should go. The first attempt to express the law is to say, "The farther out it goes, the more it makes the arm of the balance go down. So, if you want to make a heavier thing balance a lighter one that's way out near the edge, you have to put the heavier one closer to the fulcrum." The subject is discovering relations between relations: between *heavier-than* and *closer-to*, and *lighter-than* and *farther-away*, or how changes in weight and changes in distance are related.

Seriating by "inching up" or "inching down" is an operation useful in establishing equilibrium in many different kinds of systems. For example, one fifth-grade class was working on mixture problems in connection with a temperature unit. One problem was to find the temperature of water that was equal parts of 70° water and 10° water. The problem is one of ratio and proportion involving operations that have their origins in simple seriation, of being able to order a series in ascending and descending sequence. We can inch up a bit in one part of a system but keep the same ratio of one part to another by inching down in the other part of the system at the same time. Through successive steps of inching up and inching down we arrive at a limit where the two subsystems meet.

The experimenter reports on how some fifth-grade students used seriation to solve the water-mixture problem:

> While I expected many fifth graders to solve the problem of predicting the temperature of a mixture of 70° water and 10° water by an inching up and inching down, or degreeing up and degreeing down, as we called it, this experimental group did not recognize the problem as one that could be solved by seriation, and so the next lesson was designed to have children

work out a ratio problem concretely. Children were given a vertical line graph which they were to imagine was a thermometer and Cuisinaire rods, each of which they were to imagine was one degree. They were asked to work out a plan using the rods to find temperatures of specified mixtures. This activity appeared to be effective in developing the concept of a 1-to-1 ratio; children explained their strategies in terms of: "This side gives up one and that side gets one." "You degree down one and then you degree up one." They rather quickly learned to find the midpoint by using the rods. Some discarded the rods and used only the lines on the graph to arrive at an answer. Some were even degreeing up and down by 5 and 10 points at a time by the end of the lesson. However, for some children, the rods provided an essential physical referent for developing the notion of seriation.

In subsequent lessons, we worked on problems of a 2-2 or 3-3 ratio. These were easy for the children; they readily saw that a 1-1, 2-2 and other similar ratios would all produce the same results. Each time, they were asked to fill in data sheets showing how many degrees there were between hot and cold, and how this difference would be divided up for a 1-1, 2-2 ratio.

The last problem in this particular series of lessons involved unequal ratios—mixtures of 1-2, 1-3, 2-1 and 3-1 parts of hot to cold water. The teaching procedure was the same in each case: presentation of the problem and prediction as to outcome; carrying out the mixture activity and recording data; working out a solution using the Cuisinaire rods and discussion of strategies for finding solutions. Again, the rods made possible a physical representation of a 1-2 ratio; again, some children were able to abandon the rods and proceed to find solutions using the line graphs only. As one would expect, the children made slower progress on such problems than on those involving equal ratios, but all solved the problems correctly, though at different levels of abstraction.

It is often necessary not only in science and mathematics but also in the social sciences to arrange elements in some kind of order to show relations between relations. While there is no "hard" evidence to support their conviction, many teachers of older children feel that problems having to do with relations between relations (problems like understanding concepts of "velocity" and "ratio," for example) present more difficulties for most students than do problems involving classification. Many such problems have their roots in seriation activities, and, indeed, problems of ratio and proportion can be solved, though somewhat laboriously, as illustrated above, by seriating. Where seriation structures are adequate, the more difficult concepts that depend upon seriation are easier to grasp. Hence, early training in this area would seem to be critical.

HOW SERIATION DEVELOPS IN EARLY CHILDHOOD

Piaget and his co-workers have studied systematically the development of seriation in young children. They find that seriation exists at the sensorimotor level, although the behavior is unsystematic. By eighteen months, using trial-and-error procedures, the child can build a tower made of several blocks of decreasing size. By two years of age, the child can solve a problem with Montessori nesting boxes in the same fashion.

The solution to seriation problems, according to Piaget, is not merely perceptual; he finds in seriating behavior evidence of logical structure which goes beyond the perceptual. He and Inhelder describe an experiment which has bearing on this point:

> We presented children aged 4-10 with a variety of serial arrangements of sticks of different lengths. Some of these had equal differences so that the series went up in a straight line, while others had unequal differences. But these were still regular: when the sticks were ordered along a straight line, the tops of the sticks described either a positively accelerated or a negatively accelerated parabola, i.e., the differences increased regularly from left to right or they decreased regularly. The operative question is to ask the subject to compare the differences between two pairs of adjacent elements. The first pair is near the beginning of the series while the second is near the end. Now younger children (5-7 years) need to compare the two differences by measuring one pair against the other, while older children (9-10 years) can tell at once whether the differ-

ences are equal or unequal by taking the configuration of the
series into account (i.e., by referring to the shape of the line
across the top). Now this experiment seems to prove that children do not use the configuration of the whole until a compara-
tively late age. (p. 248)

In still another experiment (Inhelder and Piaget, 1964), children from 4 to 8 years of age were presented with 10 small rods
ranging from 9-12 cm., together with a set of rods of intermediate
lengths, to be inserted in the first series. The children were asked
to arrange the rods in order. The experimenters found that most
four- and five-year-olds either made no attempt to seriate or could
arrange only sub-series of 2, 3, or 4 elements. Some five-year-olds
(12%) and six-year-olds (25%) succeed by trial and error, but it is
not until seven or eight years of age that success is achieved by
means of what Piaget calls the "operational" methods, although
younger children succeed if there are only a few items and the differences in size are gross. The age at which seriation becomes operational is roughly the same age as that for the emergence of true
classification.

By the "operational" method, Piaget means that the child has
some anticipatory scheme for arranging objects in a series. In the
case of the rods, the child deliberately chooses the smallest element and proceeds to build a series in which each object is larger
than the preceding ones. This systematic method implies reversibility; finding the smallest object and then the next smallest of
those that remain means that the child must keep in mind that the
object he chooses is both longer than the one already chosen and
shorter than any that are left.

It is interesting to note that children can draw a series of rods
ranging in height from lower to higher at an earlier age than they
can do an actual seriation. Piaget's explanation of the fact that a
correct solution to drawing the series precedes success with the
rods themselves is that a drawing does not demand reversibility.
The child does not need to think, "I must find a rod which is longer
than this one but shorter than any of the others"; he draws the rods
one after another simply following one direction of the size variable. The relation that he imposes is one-directional and, therefore,

irreversible. He does not need to coordinate the two directions of looking backward and looking forward. The child anticipates the final result but not the steps needed to reach it.

More involved than simple seriation with only one variable (like length of rod) is seriation with two variables. A calendar is one example. A day can be a day of the month, part of a monthly series: 1, 2, 3, 4, etc.; and a day can also be a day of the week, as Sunday, Monday, Tuesday, etc. It is because a day possesses these two properties that it is possible to construct a table, or calendar, in which the numbers in the vertical column (usually) are all the same day of the week, and the numbers in the horizontal row are all the days in a particular week. The result is a matrix with the series ordered along both horizontal and vertical axes.

In a comparable Piagetian task, the child is presented with drawings of leaves ordered according to size and according to color intensity, with seven different sizes and seven shades, from yellow-green to dark green. The child is asked to arrange these elements as he wishes and may be given a "start" by the experimenter in the way of constructing the first row. At five years of age, children do not seriate at all; a protocol from Inhelder and Piaget (1964) describes typical behavior with a set of 32 elements:

> Hen (5;5).* The small set of 32 elements: he starts by aligning the 32 leaves, with the identical elements next to one another. He also has the 8 largest leaves together but the remaining 24 are dispersed irregularly. Can you do better still?—(He arranges them again, and ends with four collections based on size, but these are not in serial order; he ignores colour altogether.)—Can you put them together so that one can see which are dark, less dark, light and very light?—(He attempts a seriation, but this remains approximate because he is distracted by the sizes.)—Try to arrange them now so that the large ones are together and the small ones too, but so that the same colours are together as well.—(He constructs a large circle by combining the leaves by their colour, and then subdividing these col-

---

* Piaget refers to subjects by the first syllable of their name; *Hen,* for example, might stand for *Henri.* The numbers in parentheses refer to the age of the child. *Hen* is 5 years, 5 months of age.

lections according to size.)—The experimenter then fills in the top row and the left-hand column of the 16-cell matrix and asks Hen to place two or three leaves in the right cells. He can do this by trial-and-error: *because it's the same colour and the same size.* (p. 270)

Other children in the same age group, when given a hint as to how to seriate by size are able to arrange the leaves by size, but colors are distributed at random. When asked, "And where are the light ones, the dark ones, the darkest ones? Can you arrange the leaves to help find them quickly?" the child might then proceed to seriate by color but lose sight of size. Behavior at this level is consistent with what Piaget has described in connection with other tasks; the pre-operational child attends to only one variable. Just as he cannot coordinate a change in height of water level with a change in width in a conservation problem, so he cannot coordinate changes in one variable in a seriation problem with changes in another variable.

At the concrete level, protocols reveal that the child *can* take into account two variables and can complete the matrix for both color and size successfully, as the following example shows:

> Mar (7;4). Tell me what you see.—*There are some which are darker and some which are smaller than others.*—Can you put them in order?—(He takes the darkest leaves and seriates them by size.) *It's the darkest ones which I've put first.* Does it matter? (He places leaves on one another to assess their sizes, continuing with the less dark ones, etc., until the matrix is complete.—How did you arrange them so well?—*I kept looking at the smallest ones and the lightest ones.* (p. 275)

The reader will note similarities here between mental processes involved in seriation and those in classification. In each case there is anticipation or foresight of what is to come and hindsight on what has happened. As Piaget points out, classification and seriation are logical structures characterized by precise laws, like the structure of reversibility. One must be able to compare differences by going backward and forward in one's mind both as one classifies and as one seriates.

There are still more complex operations that Piaget has identified in seriation. One involves the ability to transpose differences between two items in a series to other items in the series ($A >^* B$; $B > C$; therefore $A > C$). In Piagetian terms, the relationship is "transitive," meaning that the relation between the first and second elements and the second and third, in any series, implies that the first element is in relation to the third, as the relation "greater than," "less than," or "equal to." In one experiment, the child is shown two upright rods (A and B) that differ almost imperceptibly in height. He is asked to make a comparison to see whether one is taller, or if they are the same height. He finds that B is shorter. Then the B stick is carried to another table and placed alongside another, shorter rod (C) and the child is again asked to make a size discrimination. When the child has established that $A > B$ and $B > C$, the child is asked to compare (in his head) A and C and decide whether one is taller, or if both are the same size. To solve the problem, the child must "see" B as a middle term; knowing how both A and C compare with B, he can then say, "If A is bigger than B and B is bigger than C, then A must be bigger than C," or words to that effect.

Transitivity enters into all measurement problems. One problem presented to children in Geneva involves measurement of area. The subject is presented with a number of objects: a rectangle, some small squares, and some small triangles. He is to use these to decide which of two figures, a large triangle and an irregularly-shaped figure, is the larger. A unit for measuring is provided in the form of one-half-inch-square cards. There are enough measuring cards to completely cover the irregularly-shaped object and more than enough to cover the triangle. The problem to be investigated is: at what age do children discover that it is possible to use the smaller cutouts as a common measure? At what age does the child first recognize transitivity—that one can apply a square of paper to the triangle, and alter its position on the triangle by applying the square elsewhere, with the knowledge that the space covered by the square in its new position will be equal to the same amount of space as was covered in the old position. If $A = B$, and $B = C$, then $A = C$.

The beginnings of transitivity occur in "body transfer," when the subject uses part of his own body as a *middle term* between

---

* The symbol $>$ means "greater than."

two objects. The reader will recall that one of the measurement tasks described in Chapter 5 involved the construction of a tower out of different size blocks to be matched with a tower already constructed on a lower base. To see if one tower is taller than another, the child may mark off the height of the first tower by placing his hand on his chest and, keeping his hand on his chest, compare the height of the second tower. This transitivity is at the intuitive level; operational transitivity becomes more pronounced at the next level (6 to 7 years) when a third object, similar to those under comparison and of comparable size, may be used as a transitive middle term.

In the problem of comparing the two figures, children 5 to 6 years of age typically use all the measuring cards rather than employing one as a unit. They reason that if all the cards are required to go over *B* while *A* can be covered by only some, then *A* must be smaller than *B*. Use of a common measure and recognition of its transitivity (that the segments the measure marks off will be equal because each segment is equal to the common measure) are immediate at the highest level for this task typically achieved between 8 and 9 years of age.

From the foregoing Piagetian analysis of the development and components of seriation and related activities, one can identify and arrange in order of difficulty the steps leading to operational seriation:

1. Arranging 10 or more items in a series according to one variable only
2. Arranging items in a series according to more than one variable
3. Inserting an object into an already completed series (developing concept of an inserted object as the *middle* object in a series of three, rather than as a member of a *pair* of objects)
4. Solving a double seriation matrix
5. Achievement of transitivity

PROGRAM TRAINING ACTIVITIES

The set of items developed for structured lessons for the first step in seriating—arranging items in a series according to one variable—consists of 10 cardboard cutouts of flowers in a flower pot, with each cutout varying in size almost imperceptibly. Each child is given a set with the instructions "to put the flowers in order from smallest to biggest." No attempt is made to differentiate the terms *tall* and *wide* in this first experience.

Teachers will find children's seriating behavior very much as described by Piaget. Some children (four-year-olds) cannot begin to follow the direction, "to put the flowers . . ." and need help in getting started: assistance is given in the way of placing the smallest and the largest flowers some distance apart and asking the child to place the remaining flowers "so they'll go up like steps." Children at the first level of seriation can usually proceed with the task after such assistance. However, they tend to arrange one series of three items starting with the smallest and, sometimes, another three starting with the largest, and then to place the remaining items in random fashion. The teacher then asks the child whether the flower pots "go up like steps" which is often enough of a cue so that the child, on the basis of perception, will correct his errors and complete the seriation successfully.

We are interested in using the materials, however, to train for logical operations, not perception. Given the perceptual cue of looking for a step-like arrangement, the child will continue to make mistakes, for he is not choosing a flower on the basis of its being larger than the preceding one and smaller than the one to follow. The teacher, therefore, questions the child about his choices: "Is this flower larger than the small one?" "Is it smaller than this next one?" "You have to find the one that's bigger than this one (pointing) and smaller than this one." She makes sure that the child understands the terms "smaller than" and "larger than" by showing him how to superimpose one flower upon another for a comparison of size. And, by watching the child's head and eye movements, the teacher can usually tell when the child is looking backward *and* forward as he makes comparisons. Seeing the insert as a middle term between its smaller and larger neighbors provides readiness for transitivity.

At the next level of difficulty, the materials call for the child to arrange two series of objects so that they are in one-to-one correspondence with each other. The objects in the set consist of 10 dolls

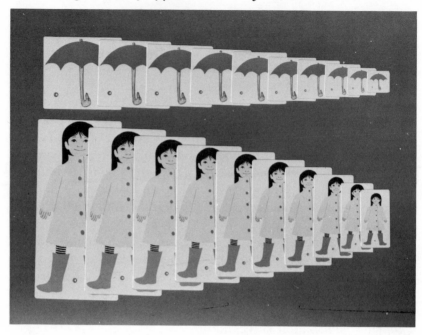

In a double seriation problem using the equipment pictured above, the child must arrange two series of objects so that they are in one-to-one correspondence with each other. As he puts the dolls and umbrellas in order of size, the child is asked to justify his choice in terms of the object being taller than the preceding one and shorter than the one to come, an activity requiring both hindsight and foresight at the same time.

and umbrellas, with dolls varying in height and umbrellas varying proportionally. The problem is to arrange the dolls in order of height and to select the proper umbrella for the doll.

The dolls, by themselves, can be used for the next step in training for seriation: insertion of a missing element. For this, after the child has completed the seriation of nine of the ten dolls, the teacher hands him one she has withheld and asks him to insert it in the proper place. This activity can be used to evaluate whether the child has made progress in considering two variables. If the child inserts the doll by considering only "smaller than," then the doll may be placed on the wrong side of the comparison doll. On the other hand, the child may just by chance insert the doll in the right place. In either case, the teacher asks the child to justify his choice: "Why do you think the doll should be there? Why did you pick that spot?" The teacher elicits further evidence of how the child is reasoning by placing the doll in the right spot (if wrong) and asking, "Could it go as well here? Why do you think so?" or by placing the doll in the wrong spot (if the child has done it right) and repeating the questions. If the child does not respond in terms of "It's smaller than this one and bigger than this one," then the teacher asks for a comparison with both neighboring dolls and makes explicit the verbal rule, "If it's smaller than this one and bigger than this one, then it's *got* to be in the right place." The verbal rule may or may not help, depending upon how far along the child is in the development of seriation, but in our experimental groups its repetition in a meaningful context enabled children to see the insert as a *middle* term of three terms, rather than as a member of a pair, an important concept, as we have seen, in the development of transitivity.

The third set of materials, a board with parallel grooves and oblong strips to fit into the grooves is designed as a practice set with built-in feedback. Since each groove will hold only the strip of the proper length, the child gets information immediately upon insertion as to whether or not his choice is correct. While some children will proceed by trial-and-error until they find the correct solution, others are obviously made more thoughtful by a negative result. Here again the teacher's questions can be worded so as to help the child think of his choice as a middle term between "taller than" and "shorter than." And, in the case of the strips, since they vary in height but not in width, the more precise terms for height are used, rather than the global, "larger," "smaller." Furthermore, color is introduced, so that children will have experience in arranging a series by a variable other than size. Each of the strips varies in the intensity of hue, so the series can be arranged from darkest to lightest, as well as from shortest to tallest. The teacher directs the children to find the "shortest, darkest one," "the tallest, lightest one," "next taller and lighter," etc., so that the two variables are identified.

These materials are also used to continue readiness training for transitivity. The verbal rule first introduced in Set 2 ("If it's smaller than this one and bigger than this one, then it's got to be in the right place) is reinforced, and for children who have mastered its application, the next step in training for transitivity is introduced. The techniques used are patterned after those by Braine (1959). First, each child is presented with two neighboring strips (A and B) in the series and asked which is shorter. The teacher uses verbal reinforcement by responding vigorously and positively to the correct response: "That's *good* thinking!" (While Braine used external reinforcement such as candy, we found in a group situation that the verbal presented fewer problems and worked effectively.) The teacher then presents another pair of strips (B and C) in the same fashion. When the child has responded correctly that A > B and B > C, the teacher says, "You've told me about these two [pointing to A and B] and these two [sliding B over to C and pointing to B and C]. Now can you tell me about these two [pointing to A and C, using hand to cover up tops of the strips where inequality is barely perceptible]." "Which is shorter, or are they the same length?" If the child does not respond correctly, the teacher raises the question as to whether B, the middle term, could be used as a common measure. Some children make use of the suggestion and move after several training sessions to a successful solution. When asked if they could be sure that A > C without measuring, they give an inferential-type response: "If this one's bigger than the second one, and the second one is bigger than the third one, then the first one's got to be bigger than the third one, too." This type of response is not forthcoming until the concrete-operational stage is reached at roughly seven years for most children, but some bright children respond in this fashion by the end of the kindergarten year.

The matrix puzzle which is next in order of difficulty calls for arranging geometric shapes in two series, according to size and according to number of sides in the shape: a triangle with 3 sides, a rectangle with 4, a pentagon with 5 and a hexagon with 6. The series arranged according to size runs horizontally, while the

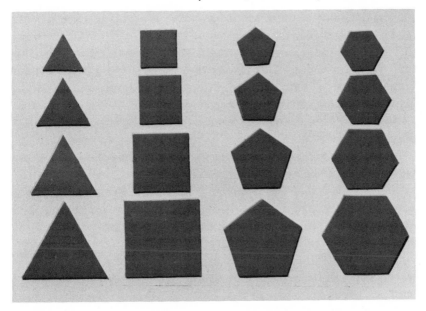

This matrix puzzle calls for arranging geometric shapes in two series: according to size, and according to number of sides to the shape. The child must keep in mind both of these variables as he arranges all 16 shapes "so that it will be easy to find the one that's smallest and has the least number of sides." In the Piagetian curriculum, the structured lessons are used for language training as well as for training in logical thinking. Here the comparative form of adjectives is emphasized.

series arranged according to number of sides runs vertically. Children first learn the names of the figures and describe how each differs from the next in the series, etc. Once perceptual details are taken care of, they are given 4 triangles ranging in size from 1″ to 3″ to seriate. This task, involving only 4 figures, is not usually difficult for the children at this stage of training. After this, the children are given four different geometric shapes, differing only in number of sides. The variable of number of sides is more difficult since it does not stand out perceptually, but it, too, can be accomplished by four-year-olds. Once these two steps are out of the way, the teacher supplies each child with all 16 figures, "to arrange so that it will be easy to find the one that's smallest and has the least number sides, or to find any other one." For children who have difficulty in getting started, the teacher may arrange the top row and left-hand column, with the rest of the rows and columns to be filled in.

As with other Piagetian activities, language plays an important part in matrix training. The child is continually called upon to explain what he is doing and why. The teacher listens to ascertain whether he is considering both size and number of sides and asks questions to call his attention to both of these variables, if the child is considering only one. Finally, the child who has solved the matrix successfully is asked to explain how he has arranged the rows and columns to another child so that the other child can carry out the same arrangement.

The final set in the Seriation Series involves measurement. While we have already devoted some attention to measurement in the Number, Measurement and Space Series, we include training here also, with special emphasis upon transitivity. The reader will recall, from the discussion in Chapter 5, that basic to the concept of measurement is the notion of a standard unit which can be transposed in space and applied as often as is necessary to whatever is to be measured. And basic to the notion of a standard unit is an awareness of the fact that one can apply the unit first on one object and then on another with the knowledge that the quantity being covered in the new position will be equal to the same quantity as was covered in the old. In other words, if $A = B$, and $B = C$, then $A = C$. The unit being applied is B; it is the middle term between A and C. Training in seriation so far has been directed toward seeing a particular object in a series as a middle term; this last activity applies earlier training to measurement.

The problem developed for this activity involves seeing which of two irregularly shaped brown and green playgrounds is larger in area, ("would have more space for children to play on"). The two playgrounds, as can be seen in the illustration, cannot be compared by superimposing one upon the other. Enough small squares and rectangles are supplied to cover the larger playground exactly and to more than cover the smaller. A correct solution again demands an inference-type thinking: "If you need all the small figures to cover the brown playground, but you don't need all to cover the green, then the brown is bigger." But to reach that level, children need to go through the intermediate steps of using *B* (the small shapes) to compare *A* (brown playground) with *B*, and of using *B* to compare *C* (green playground) with *B;* of recognizing *B* (the small shapes) as a middle term that can be used to compare *A* and *C;* and finally, of drawing the correct inference.

EPILOGUE

The curriculum activities described in these last three chapters are designed to help the child of 4 to 7 years make steady progress in the development of logical intelligence. Not all children will be able to accomplish the complete program by seven years of age; not all children reach the stage of concrete-operational thinking by seven years. But the combination of short, structured periods, plus reinforcement during periods of self-directed play will facilitate progress toward that stage and ensure that more children have the thinking skills essential for problem-solving.

REFERENCES

Beilin, H. (1965) Learning and operational convergence in logical thought development. *J. Exp. Child Psychol.*, **2**, 317-339.

Bellugi-Klima, U. (1967) The acquisition of the system of negation in children's speech. Doctoral dissertation, Harvard Graduate School of Education.

Bellugi-Klima, U., & Hass, W. (1968) Syntactical structures for modeling in preschool language training. In C. Lavatelli (Ed.), *Promising practices in language training in early childhood education.* Urbana: University of Illinois Press, ERIC Clearinghouse on Early Childhood Education.

Bereiter, C., & Engelmann, S. (1966) *Teaching disadvantaged children in the preschool.* Englewood Cliffs, N.J.: Prentice Hall.

Bernstein, B. (1961) Social class and linguistic development: a theory of social learning. In A. Halsey, J. Floud, & C. Anderson (Eds.), *Education, economy, and society.* New York: Free Press.

Blank, M., & Solomon, F. (1968). A tutorial language program to develop abstract thinking in socially disadvantaged preschool children. *Child Develpm.*, **39**, 379-390.

Bloom, B. S. (1964) *Stability and change in human characteristics.* New York: Wiley.

Bruner, J. (1964) The course of cognitive growth. *Amer. Psychologist*, **19**, 1-15.

Bruner, J., Oliver, R. & Greenfield, P., *et al.* (1966) *Studies in cognitive growth.* New York: Wiley.

Cazden, C. (1965) Environmental assistance to the child's acquisition of grammar. Doctoral thesis, Harvard University, 1965.

Clark, H. H. (1969) Linguistic processes in deductive reasoning. *Psychol. Rev.*, **76**, 387-404.

Deutsch, M., & Associates (1967) *The disadvantaged child.* New York: Basic Books.

Elkind, D. (1969) Conservation and concept formation. In D. Elkind & J. H. Flavell (Eds.) *Studies in cognitive development,* essays in honor of Jean Piaget. New York: Oxford Univ. Press, pp. 171-190.

Featherstone, J. (1968) The primary school revolution in Britain. *The New Republic,* Special Reprint, pp. 1-16.

Flavell, J., Beach, D., & Chinsky, J. (1966) Spontaneous verbal rehearsal in a memory task as a function of age. *Child Develpm.*, **37**, 283-299.

Fowler, W. (1962) Cognitive learning in infancy and early childhood. *Psychol. Bull.*, **59**, 116-152.

Greenfield, P. (1969) Teaching mathematical concepts to two-three year olds: some experimental studies. (Unpublished). Harvard University Social Relations Department.

Hart, B., & Risley, T. R. (In press) Establishing use of descriptive adjectives in the spontaneous speech of disadvantaged preschool children. *J. Applied Behavior Analysis.*

Hess, R., & Shipman, V., (1968) Parents as teachers. In C. Lavatelli (Ed.), *Promising practices in language training in early childhood education.* Urbana: University of Illinois Press, ERIC Clearinghouse on Early Childhood Education.

Hunt, J. McV. (1961) *Intelligence and experience.* New York: Ronald Press.

Inhelder, B., & Piaget, J. (1964) *The early growth of logic in the child.* New York: Harper.

Jensen, A. (1968) Social class and verbal learning. In M. Deutsch, I Katz, & A. Jensen. *Social class, race, and psychological development.* New York: Holt, Rinehart & Winston, 115-174.

Jensen, A., and Ashner, W. (1965) Syntactical mediation of serial and paired-associate learning as a function of age. *Child Develpm., 36,* 601-608.

Jensen, A. R. (1969) How much can we boost IQ and scholastic achievement? *Harvard Ed. Rev., 39,* 1-123.

Kohlberg, L. (1968) Early education: A cognitive-developmental view. *Child Develpm., 39,* 1013-1062.

Kohnstamm, G. A. (1967) *Teaching children to solve a Piagetian problem of class inclusion.* Amsterdam: North-Holland Publishing Co.

Magoun, H. W., Darling, L. & Prost, J. (1960) The evolution of man's brain. In M. Brazier, (Ed.), *The central nervous system and behavior.* Josiah Macy, Jr. Foundation.

Milner, Esther (1951) A study of the relationship between reading readiness in grade one school children and patterns of parent-child interaction. *Child Develpm.,* 1951, *22,* 95-112.

Moore, D. (In press) A critical review of methods of teaching language skills to lower class preschool children. In C. Lavatelli, Ed., *Promising practices in language training in early childhood education.* Urbana: University of Illinois Press and ERIC Clearinghouse on Early Childhood Education.

Moore, O. K. (1968) Teaching young children to read. In R. Hess & R. Bear (Eds.), *Preschool education: theory, research, and action.* Chicago: Aldine Press.

147

Piaget, J. (1950) *The psychology of intelligence*. London: Routledge & Kegan Paul.

Piaget, J. (1951) (1945, orig. French ed.). *Play, dreams, and imitation in childhood*. New York: Norton, 1951.

Piaget, J. (1952a) *The child's conception of number*. London: Routledge & Kegan Paul.

Piaget, J. (1952b) *The origins of intelligence in children*. New York: Int. Univer. Press.

Piaget, J. (1953) *How children learn from mathematical concepts. Scient. Amer.*, **189**, 74-79.

Piaget, J. (1953) *Logic and psychology*. Manchester: Manchester University Press.

Piaget, J. (1961) *Les Mecanismes perceptifs*. Paris: Presses Univer. France.

Piaget, J. (1964) Three lectures in R. E. Ripple and V. N. Rockcastle Eds.), *Piaget rediscovered*. Ithaca, New York: Cornell University Press.

Piaget, J. (1967) Notions of causality. In *Newsletter*, No. 9, Winter 1967, Science Curriculum Improvement Study, Univ. of California, Berkeley.

Piaget, J., & Inhelder, B. (1956) *The child's conception of space*. London: Routledge & Kegan Paul.

Piaget, J., Inhelder, B., and Szeminska, A. (1960) *The child's conception of geometry*. New York: Basic Books.

Ripple, R., & Rockcastle, V. (1964) (Eds.) *Piaget rediscovered: a report of the conference on cognitive studies and curriculum development*. Ithaca: School of Education, Cornell University.

Sigel, I., Roeper, A., and Hooper, F. H. (1966) A training procedure for acquisition of Piaget's conservation of quantity: a pilot study and its replication. *Brit. J. Educa. Psychol.*, **36**, 301-311.

Sinclair-de-Zwart, H. (1969) Developmental psycholinguistics. In D. Elkind & J. H. Flavell, *Studies in cognitive development*, essays in honor of Jean Piaget. New York: Oxford Univ. Press.

Skeels, H. M., & Dye, H. B. (1939) A study of the effects of differential stimulation on mentally retarded children, *Proc. Amer. Assn. Ment. Def.*, **44**, 114-136.

Slobin, D. & Welsh, C. (In press) Elicited imitation as a tool in studying language development. In C. Lavatelli (Ed.), *Promising practices in language training in early childhood education*. Urbana: University of Illinois Press and ERIC Clearinghouse on Early Childhood Education.

Smedslund, J. (1961a). The acquisition of conservation of substance and weight in children: II. External reinforcement of conservation of weight and of the operations of addition and subtraction. *Scand. J. Psychol.*, **2**, 71-84.

Smedslund, J. (1961b). The acquisition of conservation of substance and weight in children: VI. Practice on continuous versus discontinuous material in problem situations without external reinforcement. *Scand. J. Psychol.*, **2**, 203-210.

Smith, I. D. (1968) The effects of training procedures upon the acquisition of conservation of weight. *Child Develpm.*, **39**, 515-526.

Vygotsky, L. S. (1962) *Thought and language,* New York: Wiley.

Wohlwill, J. F. (1960) A study of the development of the number concept by scalogram analysis. *J. Genet, Psychol.*, **97**, 345-377.

APPENDIX 1

Syntactical Structures for
Modeling in Preschool Language Training*

THIS LISTING of syntactical structures was prepared by Dr. Bellugi-
Klima and Dr. Hass for a research project being carried out under the
auspices of the National Laboratory on Early Childhood Education.
However, a number of people have found it useful for other purposes.
Teachers who are attempting to use what might be called the "natural
method" of accelerating language development find it helpful in giving
children a language lift. The technique is relatively simple. The teacher
listens to the child and notes the immature syntactical structure that he
uses. Then she deliberately models the correct syntax and encourages
the child to use it by asking him a question, the response to which
demands use of the structure. For example, the teacher might find that
several of her students use the present tense form of verbs even when the
past tense is called for. The child might say, "Yesterday I goes to the
park and I finds a nest." The teacher says in response, "You found a nest,
Marshall? What did the nest look like? Was it a bird's nest?" Note that
the teacher has modeled for the child not only the past tense of the verb
"find" but also a transformation of the declarative present, "You find a
bird's nest," to the past interrogative, "Did you find?" She also models
the past tense of the verb "to be".

Many experts in psycholinguistics believe that the child with his
tremendous innate capacity for language will learn to speak the King's
English if he hears enough models of well spoken utterances to process
and generalize the rules. This list of syntactical structures may help the
teacher become more aware of which structures are developing during
the preschool years and enable her to help disadvantaged children to
acquire them. The examples that follow are drawn from *Teacher's Guide
to Early Childhood Curriculum: A Piaget Approach.*

* Selected on the basis of potential contribution to logical thinking.
Adapted from a list prepared by Ursula Bellugi-Klima, Salk Institute
of Biological Studies; and Wilbur Hass, University of Chicago, for ERIC
Clearinghouse on Early Childhood Education.

OUTLINE OF SYNTACTICAL STRUCTURES

Inflections

Prepositions

Auxiliary Verbs in Declarative Negative

Indirect Questions

Wh Questions

Tag Questions

Coordinations, Adversatives

Comparatives

Complex Nounphrase

Complex Auxiliary Verb

Negative and Indefinite

Sentence Connectives

    Relative Clauses

    Temporal Connectives

    Causal Connectives

    Conditional Statements

PLURALS
Some of the cars are yellow.
The beads are in the box.

REGULAR PAST TENSE
Yesterday we worked with beads.
Last time, you sorted the objects by color.

THIRD PERSON SINGULAR PRESENT INDICATIVE
The large size goes with the others.
The square fits inside the hoop.

PREPOSITIONS
Put the triangle next to the square.
Put the triangle behind the square.
Put the triangle in front of the square.

Put the penny in the cup.
Put the penny on the cup.
Put the penny under the cup.

Put the penny above the toy.
Put the penny below the toy.
Put the penny beside the toy.

Move the tree up on the paper.
Move the tree down on the paper.

Move the mat from Frank to Jim.
Move the mat to Frank from Jim.

MODALS* and "DO" WITH NEGATIVES

The cars can't be put in the same group with tools.
The daisies shouldn't go in the vase.
The squares don't cover all the space.
Three of the smallest cups don't fill the great big one.

"BE" — NEGATIVE AND QUESTION

The object is not round.
They are not things that grow.
He is not touching the other objects.
(The above could also be presented in contracted form "isn't, aren't," to correspond to the so-called negative question.)
Isn't this object round?
Aren't these things that grow?
Isn't he touching the other objects?

"BE" WITH PAST TENSE

(Use range of subjects: I, you, he, she, it, we, they, nounphrase singular, nounphrase plural.)

"BE" PAST

The umbrellas were lined up with the dolls.
I was showing you a set of beads earlier today.

"BE" PAST NEGATIVE

He wasn't using it.
We weren't looking at round objects before.

---

* *Modal* in this context refers to what is and what is not possible, or what is true or false.

152

"BE" PAST QUESTION
Weren't these the objects which could stretch?

"BE" — AFFIRMATIVE AND QUESTION
This spoon is plastic.
These sweaters are for the doll.

INDIRECT QUESTIONS
(A common error with respect to embedded questions in nonstandard speech is that word order of original question is preserved, as in: "I don't know how did I do it.")
I didn't see what you did.
Find out where you can put them.
Ask your partner how he did it.

WH QUESTIONS
(Use different interrogative words — who, what, where, when, why, how, which — and variety of auxiliary verbs — be, do, have, modals — and some negative questions.)
Which objects are made of two materials?
What can you use the long objects for?
What things can't you use for eating?
Where did you put the round objects?
Who can find the one that is different?
How could you guess which ones to use?

TAG QUESTIONS
It will look clear, won't it?
You could do it this way, couldn't you?
You could have done it a different way, couldn't you?

COORDINATIONS
Put the pennies and the toys in the box.
The red cars are parked in one field, and the blue ones in another.

ADVERSATIVES
This is tall but light.
This object is square but not large.
I am thinking of an object which is dark but not heavy.

DISJOINT
Pick out either the large ones or the dark ones.
A round piece or a square piece belongs in this pile.

COMPARATIVES
Find the larger piece.

Show me the shorter stick.
Point to the wider one.
Point to one that is longer and thinner.
Show me one which is wider and shorter.

COMPLEX NOUNPHRASE
The longer narrower stick goes here.
I am thinking of the white, square, small object.

COMPLEX AUXILIARY VERBPHRASE
We could have done it another way.
You might have sorted them like this.
This jar could have been filled with water.

NEGATION WITH INDEFINITES
None of these is round.
I don't see anything that is round.

RELATIVE CLAUSES
Whatever objects you find can be used.
What you can't sort, you can put to one side.

TEMPORAL CONNECTIVES
(Before, after, when, as soon as, etc.)
(These occur very late in the developmental sequence, and perhaps should not be used unless the children are rather advanced.)
Before you begin the game, choose a partner.
Raise your hand as soon as you have tried them all.

CAUSAL CONNECTIVES
Because this stick is the shortest, it goes on the end.

Some Piaget Tasks to Use in
Assessment of
Logical Thinking

WHILE PIAGET'S CONTRIBUTION to our understanding of the development of logical intelligence is a major one, his theory is not easy to understand and his writings are difficult. Even those writings that have been best translated are difficult. This is partly because his theory introduces many unfamiliar concepts: assimilation, accommodation, equilibration, pre-operational, concrete operations, transitivity, logical multiplication, etc. Most readers do not have referents for such concepts available to them. However, Piaget himself suggests a solution. He urges students who seek deeper insight into thinking processes to administer some of the tasks developed in Geneva and to listen carefully to children's responses.

Directions for some of the tasks follow. Two of these involve classification: *Changing Criteria* which reveals whether the child can recognize more than one property of an object, and is flexible in shifting his criterion for classifying; this task is usually passed by 75 per cent of six-year-old children; and, *Class Inclusion — Beads*, which gets at the child's ability to include a subclass in a larger class and to break the larger class down into its component parts. This task is usually passed by 75 per cent of eight-year-old children.

Two conservation tasks are included: *Conservation of Quantity* (clay) and *Conservation of Length* which reveal rather directly whether the child can reverse processes or recognize that matter or length continue to be the same unless something is added or taken away; the task of *Quantity* is usually passed at about seven years of age, and *Length* at about nine years.

Equipment needed for administration of the tasks is fairly easy to improvise. Some guidelines for assessing children's responses are included.

The reader will note that there has been no specific training of identical tasks in the program described in this volume. The tasks can therefore serve to test for transfer — that is, whether or not the training in logical thinking developed in the program transfers to other tasks requiring logical processes. Administration of the tasks at the beginning of the year and at the end will enable the teacher to judge the progress of her class, although, without the use of a control group, one cannot say to what factors the progress can be attributed.

CHANGING CRITERIA

Material:

Geometric figures cut out of construction paper:
24 circles, diameter 1 in., 12 red, 12 blue
24 circles, diameter 2 in., 12 red, 12 blue
24 squares, side 1 in., 12 red, 12 blue
24 squares, side 2 in., 12 red, 12 blue.

Presentation:

Place the figures on the table, in front of the child, without putting them into any special order. "Tell me what this is."

Part I:

Spontaneous classification.
"Can you put into piles the things that go together?"
"Put everything that is very much the same into the same piles."
"Can you separate the things that are different?"

Part II:

Dichotomy
"Now can you make just two piles and then put the things from the piles into these two boxes?"
Justification: "How did you separate them?"

Part III:

"Can you arrange the things differently and put them in two piles?" If the child reverts to his first criterion: "But you have already done that; can you find another way of putting the things together?"
Justification: "How did you separate them? Why?"

Part IV:

"Is there still another way?"
"Could you arrange these things in another way?"
If the child does not find the solution, the experimenter starts a classification by one of the two criterions that the child has not used in Part II.
"Could you continue like this? Why did I put these together in this box and the other ones in that box?"
Once the child has finished the classification:
Justification: "Why did you arrange them like this? What would you call these?"

156

CLASS INCLUSION
Hierarchy of Classes

Material:

A box with 18 wooden beads colored yellow and 2 colored red.

Presentation:

Show the box of beads to the child and ask: "What are these?" "Do you think all the yellow beads are of wood? Do you think the red beads are wood?"

Part I:

"In this box, would you say that there are more yellow beads or are there more beads made of wood?"
Justification: "Why? How do you know?"

Part II:

"There are two little girls who would like to make necklaces out of these beads. One would like first to make a necklace out of the yellow beads, and then, when she gives the beads back to me, the other girl would like to use the wooden beads. Which of the two necklaces will be longer?"
Justification: "Why?"

Part III:

a) "If you give me all the yellow beads, what will be left in the box?"
b) "If you give me all the wooden beads, will there be any beads left in the box?"
Justification: "Why? How do you know?"

Part IV:

Repeat Part I.

CONSERVATION OF LENGTH
Evaluation of the length of staggered lines

Material:

Four (4) ¼ inch square sticks; two 6 inches long, one 5 inches long, one 7 inches long.

Presentation:

"From the sticks, choose the two that are the same length." "Why didn't you choose this one (longer) and that one (shorter)?"
If the child does not appear to understand the concept of length, the problem can be put to him this way: Put two sticks of equal length in front of the child with a doll at the tip of each of the sticks. Ask the child if the two dolls will

157

have to walk the same distance to reach the end.
Justification: "Why?" . . . NB: Use dolls if necessary through all parts of the experiment.

Part I:

Arrange both sticks parallel with a distance of 2 inches separating them. Be certain that one end does not extend farther than the other.
Now move the stick that is farthest from the child 2 inches beyond the tip of the second stick to the right, and be sure to maintain the parallelism between the two sticks.
"Are both sticks the same length?" "Is one longer than the other?"
Justification: a) "How do you know?" "Tell me again, which one is longer?"
b) (only if the child reports different lengths) "If you would measure them, would they still be different lengths?"
After the child has answered put the first stick back to its original position.

Part II:

Proceed in the same way as in Part I, but this time shift the top stick to the left.

Part III:

Move (simultaneously) the first stick to the left and the second stick to the right so that the extensions added together are about one-third the length of one stick (i. e., 2 inches on either side)
Ask the same questions as in Part I.

Reference:

Piaget, J., Inhelder, B., and Szeminska, A. (1960) *The child's conception of geometry.* New York: Basic Books.

CONSERVATION OF QUANTITY

Material:

A ball of clay.

Presentation:

Give the child a ball of clay and ask him to make another exactly like it — just as big and just as heavy.

Activity:

After the child has done the activity, retain one of the balls as a standard of comparison. Change the other one by stretching it into a sausage, flattening it into a cake, or cutting it into smaller pieces. Ask if the amount of clay, its weight, and its volume have changed or remained invariant (i.e., conserved) as a result of the transformation. "Do the two pieces of clay have the same amount of clay?"
Justification: "How do you know?"

Reference:

Flavell, J. H. (1963) *The developmental psychology of Jean Piaget.* New Jersey: Van Nostrand.